# Healing Miracles of Jesus

Dr. Daniel Kazemian

NEW HARBOR PRESS

*RAPID CITY, SD*

Copyright © 2019 by Daniel Kazemian

All rights reserved. No part of this publication may be reproduced, distributed or transmitted in any form or by any means, including photocopying, recording, or other electronic or mechanical methods, without the prior written permission of the publisher, except in the case of brief quotations embodied in critical reviews and certain other noncommercial uses permitted by copyright law. For permission requests, write to the publisher, addressed "Attention: Permissions Coordinator," at the address below.

Kazemian/New Harbor Press
1601 Mt Rushmore Rd, Ste 3288
Rapid City, SD 57701
www.newharborpress.com

Ordering Information:
Quantity sales. Special discounts are available on quantity purchases by corporations, associations, and others. For details, contact the "Special Sales Department" at the address above.

Healing Miracles of Jesus/ Daniel Kazemian. -- 1st ed.
ISBN 978-1-63357-213-3

Scripture quotations marked NKJV are taken from the New King James Version®. Copyright 1982 by Thomas Nelson, Inc. Used by permission. All rights reserved.

# Contents

Introduction .......................................................... 1

What Is A Miracle? ................................................ 5

Miracles in the Old Testament ........................... 9

Miracles Recorded ............................................... 13

Healings Recorded ............................................... 77

The Reason for Infirmity ................................... 93

Miracles in the New Testament ..................... 105

Miracles Resurrection ....................................... 121

Healing of Jesus ................................................. 127

The Twelve Disciples Chosen ......................... 153

Healing & Miracles of the Apostles ................ 161

Healing Scriptures in the Old Testament ...... 193

Healing Scriptures in the New Testament .... 199

How Can We Receive Healing? ...................... 205

How to become a Christian? ........................... 209

Conclusion .......................................................... 213

About the Author ............................................... 217

# Introduction

I BELIEVE MANY GREAT stories of God's majestic will bring to you with a word of encouragement about the healing. We will be studying the healing miracles of Jesus in many places in the Bible.

We have to recognize that healing is God's will for every person who believes in the name of Jesus. We will see how God can hear the prayer of His people from Genesis to Revelation.

How God would bring hope from disease conditions to heal and will be manifested in our lives. We study that no one could do anything about the illness, but Jesus took our sickness on Himself.

Because of His passion, His supremacy, and His greatness. He can work many miracles and healing today.

We will look at every miracle and healing of God in the Old Testament and the New Testament. I searched and wrote a brief summary of every story, according to the Word of God.

It will be a clear understanding of some miracles and healing we have heard or read before by ourselves.

It will astonish us and refreshing our spirit to learn about the fascinating stories of God's wonders. A significant part of Jesus' ministry engaged to go among the people.

He laid hands on the sick; He restored the blind eyes. He touched the deaf and casting out devils. Jesus set every person free who came to Him, asking for miracles. He did because of His love and tender heart toward us.

God wants to involve Himself in people's lives, and some get sick because of disobedience to God. Some have sinned against God in the past. Some didn't follow God's plan and God's direction.

They received infirmity from rebellious hearts. God is the God of justice, and He made everything pleasant according to His plan. If we walk in His Will, we shall live in health, in peace, in prosperity, and with the joy of the Lord.

We all can get healed and restored only in the name of Jesus. When I minister and praying for healing, many individuals ask me, **"Is it God's will that I would get healed?"**

I would say with confidence, **"Yes, it is God's will that you shall get healed."** Because the Lord Jesus paid the price for our sins and sickness on the cross. Our distrust or worry can be obstacles to the phenomenon of God's healing.

I can identify these healing miracles in so many places in the Bible. Jesus's healing is available for anyone who believes in the name of the Lord and received by faith today.

Healings have happened in the time of Jesus, also after Jesus ascends to heaven. When he walked among us, He saw the desperate people needed hope and new life.

The whole earth is required signs and wonders of miracles and healing of Jesus. Because the healing of Jesus is still working in our time.

**"Jesus is the same yesterday, today, and forever."** Hebrew 13:8, NKJV.

• CHAPTER 1 •

# What Is A Miracle?

A MIRACLE IS A fact enforced by the leading action of God's law. From the ordinary to an extraordinary will transform. We will go into describing what a miracle is?

A Miracle is when God interferes in a place or circumstance that cannot be described in experimental reasons or by individual thought. Miracle will be a spectacular triumph to make a real wonder.

A divine miracle is an operation executed by God that makes a visible distinction that confirms His work.

There is a significant meaning about a miracle and the love of God. God's divine supervision,

God's control over nature, and God's authority over His creatures.

What we believe miracles be a fact from the power of God to humanity. We all have the experience that the Bible is full of wonders of God start from the Old Testament to the New Testament.

We believe throughout the Bible that God did miracles all the time. We studied that God worked out one miracle to another wonder.

We will learn as God proves His truth to His chosen people, and also, He reveals Himself to other nations. We, as Christians, believe that God does miracles to serve us and for our favor.

When God showed His miracles, He performed through His servants, His messengers, His prophets, His angels. Even though through nature and everything around.

So, with the primary purpose of demonstrating His power to bring Glory to Himself. When we glance at any situation in our lives, there is someone else who is Almighty God will control it.

It will move to the next position without authority any superpower force of man and beyond the power of man's made technology.

One of the fundamental questions that we, as believers, ask ourselves; **"sign and wonder can happen today in our present time?"**

I would answer precisely. It is the scriptural fact that God will never change. That's the experience we testify of His mercy, and we believe it, and we know the Word is the truth, and we see the Glory of God is around us all the time.

The thought is if God showed surprise to His people in the past, He did on many occasions. He operates His power by no one's permission. His nature and His character have divinely performed wonders for the entire world.

Miracles have established an eternal mission; they will be carried out to bring the manifestation of the existence of God. His presence covers the whole earth; His miracles and healing bring honor and Glory to Himself.

• CHAPTER 2 •

# Miracles in the Old Testament

THE ACTUAL REASON FOR the wonders, miracles in the Old Testament is to confirm God's presence and His existence before the foundation of the world.

His mighty spirit and His authority make His creation to completion, but still to show His mercy for humankind never changes.

It is, therefore, no wonder that the Old Testament reveals all authorities of God from:
- **Death to life,**
- **Sickness to healing,**
- **Poverty to prosperity,**
- **Failure to victory.**

As we acknowledge Him, He is a magnificent God, and nothing will take place without God's divine involvement and being fully engaged.

We will be looking at the miracle and healing of God in the Old Testament; then, we will be learning many wonders of God in Jesus.

We will be viewing from many different situations like; **'events, stories, war, nature, the human condition, and healing of any disease.'**

A unique act is manifesting spiritual interference in individual circumstances. It describes miracles as miraculous demonstrations of the supernatural authority of God in our world.

The manifestation of God's miracles is chosen by Him. He who entrusted His Son Jesus to accomplish them for His honor.

We all have noticed many people having doubts about the wondrous miracle and powerful healings of Jesus.

Some have made their mind reject the existence of God who is the Maker of all things without Him nothing has been created.

His power made a perfect act on every creation to function for the Glory of God.

The Word said: **"Heaven is my throne, and the earth is my footstool."** Isaiah 66:1, NKJV.

An action that appears mysterious by the rule of nature, and it operates as to be a majestic source an act of God.

These are the evidence of God's working power has performed by the mighty Hand of God. We see God was setting up His plan to do the miraculous in seven days of His creation.

God was always at work doing a miracle in every area of human life. Some people have seen, but some people couldn't see the work of God with their natural eyes.

Because we believe God, but some don't believe it. They couldn't see anything of the miraculous power of His Glory. God revealed Himself to humanity, and we know God is the Spirit.

No man can see God with natural eyes. We can see only God with the Spiritual eyes in Jesus when we accept Him as our Lord and Savior.

There will be a situation that will occur in nature, and human life is out of control of man's power. The intensity miracles confirm the majesty and power of God..

A miracle is a phenomenal demonstration of God's authority in which He involves in human relations.

Miracles represent God's dominance, serving His amazement to His children, and carry out as signs to explain who God is!

• CHAPTER 3 •

# Miracles Recorded

**The Story of Creation:**
IN THE CREATION, GOD spoke to everything out of nothing into existence. This first action of God was genuinely authoritative.

The purpose of all events that happen entirely is the power of God. The evidence of the miracle of creation that God is the Creator characterizes as the perfect God.

It relates the act of creation to the three Persons manifested in One Godhead called: **Trinity.**

- God the Father is as the Creator.
- God the Son is as the Savior.
- God the Holy Spirit is as the Teacher, Guider, Comforter.

God's creations have finished, according to God's word. He formed the work of His creation, which is He enjoyed within six days.

Then God rested in seven days, and He blessed the Sabbath day.

- **First-Day:** *"Then God said, "Let there be light"; and there was light. And God saw the light, that it was good; and God divided the light from the darkness. God called the light Day, and the darkness He called Night. So, the evening and the morning were the first day."* Genesis 1:3-5, NKJV.

- **Second-Day:** *"Let there be a firmament in the midst of the waters, and let it divide the waters from the waters."* Genesis 1:6-8, NKJV.

- **Third-Day:** *"God called the dry land Earth, and the gathering together of the waters He called Seas. And God saw that it was good."* Genesis 1:9-10, NKJV.

  *"Let the earth bring forth grass, the herb that yields seed, and the fruit tree that yields fruit according to its kind, whose seed is in itself, on the earth; and it was so."* Genesis 1:11-13, NKJV.

- **Fourth-Day:** *"Let there be* lights in the firmament of the heavens *to divide the day from the night; and let them be for signs and seasons, and for days and years; and let them be for lights in the firmament of the heavens* to give light on the earth; *and it was so."* Genesis 1:14-19, NKJV.
- **Fifth-Day:** *"Let the waters abound with* an abundance of living creatures, *and* let birds fly above the earth *across the face of the firmament of the heavens."* Genesis 1:20-23, NKJV.
- **Sixth-Day:** *"Let the earth bring forth the living creature according* to its kind: cattle and creeping thing and beast of the earth, *each according to its kind; and it was so."* and *"*Let Us make man in Our image, *according to* Our likeness; *let them have dominion over the fish of the sea, over the birds of the air, and the cattle, over all the earth and over every creeping thing that creeps on the earth. So, God created man* in His own image; *in the image of God He created him; male and female He created them."* Genesis 1:24-31, NKJV.
- **Seventh-Day:** *"Thus, the heavens and the earth, and all the host of them were finished.*

*And on the seventh day, God ended His work which He had done, and He rested on the seventh day from all His work which He had done. Then God blessed the seventh day and sanctified it, because in it He rested from all His work which God had created and made."* Genesis 2:1-3, NKJV.

**Noah's Flood experience:**

There was the violent population is becoming progressively worse that was growing upon the earth.

There is a man named Noah, who was righteous and had a favorite in the eyes of God. He saw the world became wicked and cruel.

He sent punishment and judgment upon the earth by the flood. He gave sustaining grace to Noah and his family.

The reason for this judgment was the evil and outrageous corruption that covered the earth came from the generation of Adam.

God chose to wipe out the human race with all of the ungodly people. There was one ordinary man Noah with his family who was living in an evil society. But he remained faithful and devoted to God.

There was a flood throughout the earth, a catastrophic disaster event of the entire planet by the plan of God.

The flood destroyed the whole world entirely. The excellent safety of Noah's family of eight were upright people with all their creatures in the Ark. God guided them; the Ark landed, and they were inhabiting.

**"So, the Lord said, "I will destroy man whom I have created from the face of the earth, both man and beast, creeping thing and birds of the air, for I am sorry that I have made them." But Noah found grace in the eyes of the Lord."** Genesis 6:7-8, NKJV.

**Confusion of Languages:**

As we see at the Tower of Babel, there was a worldwide of one language immediately transferred into many languages.

After the flood, as the human population rapidly increased, this action assigned by God brought confusion in their communications.

It was the absolute purpose of the initial separation of humankind to scatter them throughout the earth, and their breakup into different races and cultures.

**"Come, let Us go down and there confuse their language, that they may not understand one another's speech."** Genesis 11:1-8, NKJV.

### Sin Cities Destruction:

Sodom and Gomorrah were cities with the corruption wickedness and evil of populations were great. So, the Lord rained down Sulphur and fire from heaven on the cities by which they were wiped out. It can be found in Sulphur in the area Dead Sea today.

**"Then the Lord rained brimstone and fire on Sodom and Gomorrah, from the Lord out of the heavens."** Genesis 19:24, NKJV.

### Lot's Protection from Destruction:

Lot had obtained miraculous salvation from Sodom. Two angels came to Lot to warn him to escape the city that God's wrath will destroy the city. Genesis, chapter 19. Lot's wife disobeyed by being turned into a pillar of salt.

**"But his wife looked back behind him, and she became a pillar of salt."** Genesis 19:26, NKJV.

### Isaac Conception:

God has promised to Abraham to have a son will be a divine conception. He was 100-year-old that his wife would carry a son. Although Sarah was very aged, she conceived and bared a son.

They loved him and named him Isaac, and he was a miracle Promise of God. Sarah, still as an elderly mother, was able to take care of her baby Isaac easily.

**"And the Lord visited Sarah as He had said, and the Lord did for Sarah as He had spoken."** Genesis 21:1, NKJV.

**Provision of a Ram:**

God wanted to test Abraham's faith. The next extraordinary appearance in his life was to have faith counted as righteousness that related to the command of God.

So, Abraham offered him, Isaac, as a sacrifice on a mountain of Moriah, but God saw his faithfulness, He provided a ram to sacrifice.

**"Then Abraham lifted his eyes and looked, and there behind him was a ram caught in a thicket by its horns. So, Abraham went and took the ram and offered it up for a burnt offering instead of his son."** Genesis 22:13, NKJV.

**Joseph Rescued from the Pit:**

Joseph's dreams had impacted his brothers with jealousy that he will rule over his family.

Joseph's brother throwing him into the pit then sold him into slavery.

Joseph was brought to Egypt and bought by Potiphar, later he became Pharaoh's officials' second command of authority in Egypt.

**"Then they took him and cast him into a pit. And the pit was empty; there was no water in it."** Genesis 37:24, NKJV.

**Moses in a Baby basket:**

Moses' mother gives birth to her son; she chooses to hide her baby was an enormous responsibility to protect him.

So, she sets up to put him in a basket along the surface water of the Nile River. Moses's mother had hoped that someone would find him and adopted him.

Moses's sister Miriam follows the basket to observe from near to far. The pharaoh's daughter was nearby heard the baby crying.

She looked at the basket; she wanted to keep the baby for herself. Moses grew up in the palace.

**"But when she could no longer hide him, she took an ark of bulrushes for him, daubed it with asphalt and pitch, put the child in it, and laid it**

**in the reeds by the river's bank."** Exodus 2:3, NKJV.

**Burning Bush:**

God had a plan to call Moses that he became His servant to deliver his people; they were crying out to God.

He heard their petition; He wants to prepare Moses to set His people free from Egypt. Moses was shepherding his father-in-law's sheep, in the land of Midian.

God has spoken to Moses on Mount Horeb from the fire, but the bush didn't burn. The voice of God came out of the fire bush.

**"And the Angel of the Lord appeared to him in a flame of fire from the midst of a bush. So, he looked, and behold, the bush was burning with fire, but the bush was not consumed."** Exodus 3:2, NKJV.

**Aaron's Staff Turned into a Snake:**

They enslaved all Israelites in Egypt, God chooses Moses to send him to Pharaoh. They went to Pharaoh, and he asked; show me a miracle.

Aaron's staff turned into a serpent and changed back to the Staff again. It was under God's authority in the presence of the Pharaoh.

**"For every man threw down his rod, and they became serpents. But Aaron's rod swallowed up their rods."** Exodus 7:12, NKJV.

**The Ten Plagues:**

Moses asked Pharaoh to **"Let my people go,"** he refused it. God assured Moses that he would show his power to convince Pharaoh.

God would harden his heart, making him stubbornly against the Israelites, not leaving the land.

Later he would show up a list of plagues with the growing condition of being severe that ended up with the death of every firstborn male in Egyptian.

**1. Water to Blood:**

As **the first plague** started, Aaron's staff touched the Nile River, the water turned into blood.

The water blood was in every place, could not drinkable, all fish died, and it held the air with a horrible smell.

"Then the Lord spoke to Moses, Say to Aaron, 'Take your rod and stretch out your hand over the waters of Egypt, over their streams, over their rivers, over their ponds, and over all their pools of water, that they may become blood. And there shall be blood throughout all the land of Egypt, both in buckets of wood and pitchers of stone." Exodus 7:19, NKJV.

**2. Frogs:**

It brought **the second plague** in an invasion of lots of frogs. They took place from every water source around land and overflowed the people and all around them.

"But if you refuse to let them go, behold, I will smite all your territory with frogs. So, the river shall bring forth frogs abundantly, which shall go up and come into your house, into your bedroom, on your bed, into the houses of your servants, on your people, into your ovens, and into your kneading bowls." Exodus 8:2-4, NKJV.

**3. Lice:**

God used Aaron's staff in **the third plague**; he smites the dust, and lice climbed up from the ground.

The outbreak went throughout the land around every man and creature. The Egyptians magic could not stop again.

**"So, the Lord said to Moses, Say to Aaron, 'Stretch out your rod, and strike the dust of the land, so that it may become lice throughout all the land of Egypt."** Exodus 8:16, NKJV.

### 4. Flies:

God used **the fourth plague** to involve the land of Egypt, mainly and not affected Jewish people who have lived in Goshen.

The large group of insect flies was intolerable. So, this time, Pharaoh allowed the people to go into the land with conditions to make sacrifices to God.

**"Or else, if you will not let My people go, behold, I will send swarms of flies on you and your servants, on your people and into your houses. The houses of the Egyptians shall be full of swarms of flies, and also the ground on which they stand."** Exodus 8:21, NKJV.

### 5. Deadly Disease Livestock:

God sent **the fifth plague** a fatal infection through all creatures and animals. It's killed and affecting only the livestock of the Egyptians, but Jewish's herd continued untouched.

**"behold, the hand of the Lord will be on your cattle in the field, on the horses, on the donkeys, on the camels, on the oxen, and on the sheep—a very severe pestilence."** Exodus 9:3, NKJV.

### 6. Boils:

God instructed Moses and Aaron to move on **the sixth plague**, to throw ashes into the air. It is occurring in horrible and terrible boils popping up in the land and their livestock.

The pain and suffering were so unbearable that when the Egyptian magicians with their powers sought to stop boils in front of Moses, they could not do it.

**"So, the Lord said to Moses and Aaron, take for yourselves handfuls of ashes from a furnace, and let Moses scatter it toward the heavens in the sight of Pharaoh. And it will become fine dust in all the land of Egypt, and it will cause boils that break out in sores on man and beast throughout all the land of Egypt."** Exodus 9:8-9, NKJV.

### 7. Thunder and Hail:

**In the seventh plague**, God brought rains and hail falling rapidly with a loud rumbling that killed people and animals and destroyed crops.

Although Pharaoh recognized his sin, later the storm settled down, he rejected freedom to the Jewish again.

**"Behold, tomorrow about this time I will cause very heavy hail to rain down, such as has not been in Egypt since its founding until now."** Exodus 9:18, NKJV.

### 8. Locusts:

**The eighth plague** is the locusts that would strike to be the most destructive and damaging to the land. Pharaoh saw frogs and lice were dangerous.

These insects devoured every new growing plant they could strike. Later, Pharaoh agreed to Moses that he had sinned.

**"Or else, if you refuse to let My people go, behold, tomorrow I will bring locusts into your territory."** Exodus 10:4-5, NKJV.

## 9. Darkness:

**In the ninth plague**, it was three days of absolute darkness spread over the land. The night was profound and black, and no one could see each other from far.

But it was light in the Jewish area, and they loved the light of day. So, Pharaoh sought to arrange the release of the Israelites.

He began to negotiate that the people could leave if they left their flocks behind; it could not be accepting this deal.

**"Then the Lord said to Moses, "Stretch out your hand toward heaven, that there may be darkness over the land of Egypt, darkness which may even be felt." So, Moses stretched out his hand toward heaven, and there was thick darkness in all the land of Egypt three days."** Exodus 10:21-22, NKJV.

## 10. Death of a First-Born Child:

They informed Pharaoh that the final plague would be the most destructive. God instructed the Israelites to sacrifice lambs, and they would paint the blood on their doorposts.

The Israelites observed these orders and still requested to get all the jewelry, gold, silver, and dresses from the Egyptians. The Israelites would later use these treasures for the tabernacle.

At midnight, an angel showed up and passed over all the Israelites homes with the blood of the lambs.

But every Egyptian family had a firstborn child who would die, including Pharaoh's son too.

It's created such an outcry that Pharaoh directed all Israelites to leave the land and take everything that they owned.

**"Then Moses said, Thus says the Lord: About midnight I will go out into the midst of Egypt; and all the firstborn in the land of Egypt shall die, from the firstborn of Pharaoh who sits on his throne, even to the firstborn of the female servant who is behind the handmill, and all the firstborn of the animals."** Exodus 11:4-5, NKJV.

**Moses Divided the Red Sea:**

After Moses, along with all Israelites left Egypt, Pharaoh began to chase them to bring them back. God directed them to approach the Red Sea.

God allowed Moses to separate the waters so the people could carefully cross through the dry ground. At the same time, the army of Pharaoh trying to cross the Red Sea, which they were chasing the people.

As quickly as they passed it through, the Lord ordered Moses to reach out his hand so the waters could rush back. Therefore, they drowned underwater the full army of Pharaoh.

**"And the Lord said to Moses, Why do you cry to Me? Tell the children of Israel to go forward. But lift up your rod, and stretch out your hand over the sea and divide it. And the children of Israel shall go on dry ground through the midst of the sea."** Exodus 14:13-28, NKJV.

**Sweet Water:**

So, Moses cried out to the Lord God for guidance, and the Lord appeared to him a piece of wood. Moses threw it into the water, made it sweet to drink.

**"So, he cried out to the Lord, and the Lord showed him a tree. When he cast it into the waters, the waters were made sweet. There He made a statute and an ordinance for them, and there He tested them."** Exodus 15:25, NKJV.

**Receiving Manna from Heaven:**

They assumed all Israelites about to starve to death. The Lord appeared to Moses that by His glory, He would send them plenty of Manna from heaven to feed them.

The Lord has taken care of them for forty years in the desert until they arrived in Canaan.

The Word of God said: Manna sent down from heaven; it was manifesting God's presence. God prepared the Israelites to trust God.

**"Then the Lord said to Moses, behold, I will rain bread from heaven for you. And the people shall go out and gather a certain quota every day, that I may test them, whether they will walk in My law or not."** Exodus 16:4, NKJV.

**Quails Brought Food:**

To provide food for the camp, as God has promised Moses to provide food for His people.

The Lord used a massive quail; they came in the evening and covered the whole camp with the blessings of God. They brought provisions like a meat to the children of Israel.

**"So, it was that quail came up at evening and covered the camp, and in the morning the dew lay all around the camp."** Exodus 16:13, NKJV.

**Water Comes Out of the Rock:**

Moses strikes the rock with his rod, and the water was poured out in extreme plenty, like floods and streams for the thirsty people, and their flocks too.

**"Behold, I will stand before you there on the rock in Horeb; and you shall strike the rock, and water will come out of it, that the people may drink."** Exodus 17:6, NKJV.

**Moses Lifted His Hands:**

On the battlefield, Moses stands on the top of the hill and lifting his hands for those soldiers to win the battle.

God brings victory, not because of the courage of the soldiers and not to depend on the intelligence of the ruling general.

Because of a man who trusts in God to become a leader of prayer and intercession in the time of war.

**"And so, it was, when Moses held up his hand, that Israel prevailed; and when he let down his hand, Amalek prevailed. But Moses' hands became heavy; so, they took a stone and put it under him, and he sat on it. And Aaron and Hur supported his hands, one on one side,**

**and the other on the other side; and his hands were steady until the going down of the sun. So, Joshua defeated Amalek and his people with the edge of the sword."** Exodus 17:11-13, NKJV.

**Thunder and Lightning on Mount Sinai:**

There were thunder and lightning with a cloud of smoke over the mountain. The sound of a trumpet was loud that the people were trembling.

Then Moses brought the people out of the camp to stand near the mountain and was covered with smoke. The Lord called Moses to meet Him up the mountain.

**"Then it came to pass on the third day, in the morning, that there were thunderings and lightnings, and a thick cloud on the mountain; and the sound of the trumpet was very loud, so that all the people who were in the camp trembled."** Exodus 19:16-20, NKJV.

**The Pillar of Cloud:**

At the time, Exodus of the children of Israel leaving the land of Egypt. They needed the most guidance from God evermore.

They didn't know where they were traveling in the desert by day or night. There was not any sign to lead them in the right direction to the Promise's Land.

The Lord has manifested His presence and His Glory as the God of Israel to His people.

According to Exodus, the pillar of the cloud was watching over the Israelites and guide them. The pillar of cloud settled and stayed at the door of the tabernacle, and the Lord spoke to Moses.

All the people who looked at the pillar of the cloud remain at the tabernacle door, and all the people in their tent door praised and worshiped.

**"And the Lord went before them by day in a pillar of cloud to lead the way, and by night in a pillar of fire to give them light, so as to go by day and night. He did not take away the pillar of cloud by day or the pillar of fire by night from before the people."** Exodus 13:21-22, NKJV.

**The Cloud as God's Glory:**

The cloud represents the Glory of God, and it's said: the cloud covered the tabernacle of meeting.

Even when Moses could not enter the tabernacle of meeting, the Glory filled and rested upon the tabernacle. When the priests came out, and the Glory of the Lord filled the house of God.

**"Then the cloud covered the tabernacle of meeting, and the glory of the Lord filled the tabernacle. And Moses was not able to enter the tabernacle of meeting, because the cloud rested above it, and the glory of the Lord filled the tabernacle."** Exodus 40:34-35, NKJV.

### Moses' face Shines:

When God called Moses to come up to meet God, he stood face-to-face with God on the mount of Sinai.

He spent time in God's presence after He handed over the two tablets of the Testimony, then Moses came down from mount Sinai.

He called Aaron and all Israelites, all rulers of the Congregations, to speak with him that he brought the message of God for them.

They realized the face of Moses was shining and glowing brightly. They couldn't stand to be near to him because Moses met God face to face.

They knew he met the Lord, and he veiled his face. Anytime he entered the Lord's presence, and he removed his mask to meet the Lord again.

"Now it was so, when Moses came down from Mount Sinai (and the two tablets of the Testimony were in Moses' hand when he came down from the mountain), that Moses did not know that the skin of his face shone while he talked with Him." Exodus 34:29-35, NKJV.

**Death of Nadab and Abihu:**

The sons of Aaron were Nadab and Abihu to bring their offering. They took their censer, and set fire to it; they put incense on it.

Then they offered profane fire before the Lord. The Word said; it was not the command of the Lord.

So, the fire of God was sent out from His presence to consume them. The Lord struck them with His presence; they died over there.

**"Then Nadab and Abihu, the sons of Aaron, each took his censer and put fire in it, put incense on it, and offered profane fire before the Lord, which He had not commanded them. So, fire went out from the Lord and devoured them, and they died before the Lord."** Leviticus 10:1-2, NKJV.

**Aaron Offering Consumed:**

It was the time of offering to the Lord. Moses commanded Aaron to give his offering on the Alter, make atonement for himself and his people.

They killed a bull, a ram, as sacrifices for the peace offering. They killed a goat for the sin offering. They brought grain a handful of it for the grain offering burned on the altar.

After all offerings: the sin offering, the burnt offering, and peace offerings have presented on the Alter.

**"Moses and Aaron went into the tabernacle of meeting,"** Leviticus 9:23, NKJV.

They came out to bless the people. Suddenly, the fire of the Lord came out and consumed the burnt offering. People saw what happened, they shouted, they went to the knees on their faces.

**"and fire came out from before the Lord and consumed the burnt offering and the fat on the altar. When all the people saw it, they shouted and fell on their faces."** Leviticus 9:22-24, NKJV.

**Fire from the Lord:**

When the people began to complain about their hardships, the Word said: The Lord was very displeased. He sent out His fire from heaven to consume them in the whole camp.

The fire of God was among them, and the people cried out and asking Moses that he would ask God to bring the fire down.

**"Now when the people complained, it displeased the Lord; for the Lord heard it, and His anger was aroused. So, the fire of the Lord burned among them, and consumed some in the outskirts of the camp."** Numbers 11:1-3, NKJV.

**Earth Swallowed Them:**

These men Korah, Dathan, Abiram have attacked Moses and Aaron for promoting themselves over the people. They demanded Moses that they didn't believe that God has appointed Moses, so they rebelled against him.

But God-given authority to Moses and after God made a judgment against them. Moses spoke the word to all of them.

Suddenly the earth opens its mouth, and they were standing, swallows them up with all their households.

**"And the earth opened its mouth and swallowed them up, with their households and all**

**the men with Korah, with all their goods. So, they and all those with them went down alive into the pit; the earth closed over them, and they perished from among the assembly."** Numbers 16:32-33, NKJV.

### 250 Men Consumed by Fire:

These three men, Korah, Dathan, and Abiram, rose up against Moses, and they gathered 250 men with them. The Lord heard and saw them.

The Lord displeased these men were against His servant Moses. The fire of the Lord came out to consume these 250 men who were offering the incense.

**"And a fire came out from the Lord and consumed the two hundred and fifty men who were offering incense."** Numbers 16:35, NKJV.

### Plague killing 14,700 people:

The Word Said: The wrath has come out from the Lord. Aaron offered with an incense censer and made atonement for them.

Because of the plague, fourteen thousand seven hundred people died, and Moses stopped the plague.

**"Now those who died in the plague were fourteen thousand seven hundred, besides those who died in the Korah incident. So, Aaron returned to Moses at the door of the tabernacle of meeting, for the plague had stopped."** Numbers 16:46-50, NKJV.

### Aaron's Rod Budded:

God chooses who will lead the children of Israel. God told them to put a rod from each tribe and write their name on the rod. Also, put Aaron's name on the rod of Levi in the tabernacle of the meeting.

The next day Moses entered the Tabernacle, he saw Aaron's rod had grown and brought forth buds, had made blossoms, and gave ripe almonds.

**"Now it came to pass on the next day that Moses went into the tabernacle of witness, and behold, the rod of Aaron, of the house of Levi, had sprouted and put forth buds, had produced blossoms and yielded ripe almonds."** Numbers 17:2-8, NKJV.

### Struck the Rock for Water:

The people wanted water from Moses, so he lifted his hands to strike the rock twice with his staff. The stream water came out of the rock. The people drank and along with their animals too.

**"Then Moses lifted his hand and struck the rock twice with his rod; and water came out abundantly, and the congregation and their animals drank."** Numbers 20:11, NKJV.

**Fight Victory over Canaanite:**

The Canaanites who inhabited in the South, their king of Arad heard that Israel would come down to Atharim.

King Arad and his army fought against Israel, and they took many prisoners. Israel asked God and made a vow if the Lord would give them victory over the Canaanite, then they will destroy their cities as well.

The Lord listened to their petition and answered their request. They destroyed the Canaanites and their town. The place is called: Hormah.

**"And the Lord listened to the voice of Israel and delivered up the Canaanites, and they utterly destroyed them and their cities. So, the name of that place was called Hormah."** Numbers 21:1-3, NKJV.

**Complaints Turn to Fiery Snakes:**

The Israelites were in the wilderness, and they started to complain to Moses and God, why we are here in this desert. There is no food, no water, our soul dislikes and not having a real life.

So, it displeased the Lord with the people's murmuring. He sent snakes among people; they bit people all around in the camp, some people died.

The Israelites ask Moses to pray that the Lord will take away all snakes from the camp.

**"So, the Lord sent fiery serpents among the people, and they bit the people; and many of the people of Israel died."** Numbers 21:6-7, NKJV.

**Balaam's Donkey Speaks:**

An angel is sent off to a destination against Balaam to show God's anger. Balaam's donkey spoken to him and protected him again from the angel, and finally, he spoke to Balaam. He went what the angel asked him to talk to Balak's officials.

**"Then the Lord opened the mouth of the donkey, and she said to Balaam, what have**

**I done to you, that you have struck me these three times?"** Numbers 22:21-35, NKJV.

**Moses Died Directly by God:**

For the time of Moses, which the Lord has directed his life of living and serving on the earth. The Lord was ready to take him up. God gave him 120-years with a long life.

Before the Lord has shown him up the valley from his eyes that the Lord has sworn to his forefathers to have the land. The Lord said to him, and you will see the land from far.

But you will not cross over. He died in the direction of God in the land of Moab. But no one knows where his grave is to this day.

**"And He buried him in a valley in the land of Moab, opposite Beth Peor; but no one knows his grave to this day. Moses was one hundred and twenty years old when he died. His eyes were not dim, nor his natural vigor diminished."** Deuteronomy 34:6-7, NKJV.

**Jordan River Divided:**

When the priests carrying the ark of the covenant through the Jordan river, their feet touched the water's edge. The water stopped flowing so that Israel crossed over on the dry ground at a town called Adam.

**"Then the priests who bore the ark of the covenant of the Lord stood firm on dry ground in the midst of the Jordan; and all Israel crossed over on dry ground until all the people had crossed completely over the Jordan."** Joshua 3:14-17, NKJV.

### Walls of Jericho Collapsed:

Joshua and his men followed God's command to march around the city for seven days. They carried the ark of the Lord along with the seven priests who blew the trumpets.

When on the seven days Joshua ordered all men to shout and blow the trumpets, suddenly the wall of Jericho collapsed.

They took the city, and they possessed everything in it. It's the faith to obey God that makes a great miracle for us.

**"So, the people shouted when the priests blew the trumpets. And it happened when the people heard the sound of the trumpet, and the people shouted with a great shout, that the wall fell down flat. Then the people went up into the**

**city, every man straight before him, and they took the city."** Joshua 6:6-20, NKJV.

**Sun and Moon Stood Still:**

On the battlefield, God was taking care of His people to win the battle against the Amorites. When the time was near to win their fight, Joshua said to the Lord in the presence of Israel.

The sun stood still, and then the moon stopped over Gibeon. It became a more extended day to empower the Israelites to overcome a momentous battle.

God was watching over His people to show them a miracle in the middle of the day and win the victory over the enemies.

**"Then Joshua spoke to the Lord in the day when the Lord delivered up the Amorites before the children of Israel, and he said in the sight of Israel: "Sun, stand still over Gibeon; And Moon, in the Valley of Aijalon." So, the sun stood still, And the moon stopped, Till the people had revenge, Upon their enemies."** Joshua 10:12-13, NKJV.

**A Huge Hailstorm killed Amorites:**

The Azekah was the enemy of Israel, they were on the battlefield, the Azekah army fled, and going down to Bethhoron. The Lord dropped down massive, large hailstones from heaven upon them Azekah, and they all died.

**"And it happened, as they fled before Israel and were on the descent of Beth Horon, that the Lord cast down large hailstones from heaven on them as far as Azekah, and they died. There were more who died from the hailstones than the children of Israel killed with the sword."** Joshua 10:11, NKJV.

**Hollow Place in Lehi Spilled for Water:**

After Samson fought with thousand, the men of the Philistines killed them all. He called that place Ramath Lehi, and he was very thirsty; he prayed God would give him water to drink.

God answered his prayer, God split the hollow place, and water came out. He drank water and renewed his spirit and revived, called the place: En Hakkore in Lehi.

**"So, God split the hollow place that is in Lehi, and water came out, and he drank; and his spirit returned, and he revived. Therefore, he called its name En Hakkore, which is in Lehi to this day."** Judges 15:17-19, NKJV.

**Gideon's Sign of Dry Fleece:**

The people of Midianites and Amalekites were an enemy of Israel. These two enemies of Israel were trying to destroy everything in the land.

So, the people cried out to get help from the Lord. Gideon said to the Lord: if you will save Israel by my hand what you have promised.

Because of fear, they were hiding from the Midianites. The Lord said to him: The Lord is with you, Gideon wanted to know a sign from the Lord, he proposed to the Lord.

He said: I will place a fleece of wool on the threshing floor; **Let it be dry on the fleece only,** and it is dew on the ground. God did what Gideon asked for; God gave them a victory over their enemy.

**"And God did so that night. It was dry on the fleece only, but there was dew on all the ground."** Judges 6:36-40, NKJV.

**The Angel Prepares food for Gideon:**

He had to work on separating grain from wheat in the winepress. Gideon was wondering where the miracle of God coming from which their enemy tried to attack them all the time.

The angels of the Lord appeared to Gideon; He encouraged Gideon that he is a man of courage. The Lord has promised him to save His people from the Midianites.

Gideon was excited to prepare an offering to the Lord. He went to get a young goat and unleavened bread from an ephah of flour.

The Angel of the Lord said: put the meat, the unleavened bread laying down on the rock, then pour out the broth.

Gideon did; the Angel of the Lord put out his staff touched the meat and the unleavened bread.

The fire came out of the rock consumed the meat and the unleavened bread. Suddenly the angel of the Lord departed from him.

**"Then the Angel of the Lord put out the end of the staff that was in His hand, and touched the meat and the unleavened bread; and fire rose out of the rock and consumed the meat and the unleavened bread. And the Angel of the Lord departed out of his sight."** Judges 6:19-21, NKJV.

**The Angel Ascended in the Flame:**

When the angel of the Lord gave Manoah good news about his wife will deliver a chosen child who is Samson. They invited the angel to have a meal with them.

Angel of the Lord said: No, I cannot have any meal, but you may offer your burnt offering unto the Lord.

So, Manoah picked up a young goat with the grain offering. Manoah presented as an offering upon the rock to the Lord.

Meanwhile, Manoah and his wife were looking at Alter. The angel of the Lord was in the flame of the Alter and ascended into heaven. Manoah and his wife fell on their face on the ground.

**"it happened as the flame went up toward heaven from the altar—the Angel of the Lord ascended in the flame of the altar! When Manoah and his wife saw this, they fell on their faces to the ground."** Judges 13:19-20, NKJV.

**Man of God Death by the Lion:**

There was an old prophet who lived in Bethel. His sons came to tell him what they have heard about the man of God had done excellent work.

The prophet asked them which way is he going? They said he came from Judah. The prophet rode on his donkey and looking after the man of God.

The prophet found him and sitting under an oak. He asked the man of God, come with me to eat bread in my home.

The man of God said: I have told by the Word of the Lord, I cannot eat or nor drink water with you, nor going back where I came.

The prophet said to him; I am a prophet; come home with me. The man of God agreed to go to the prophet's home. They sat down in his home. After eating, the prophet prophesied to him.

Because you have disobeyed the Lord, He told you; do not eat or drink water. But you didn't keep the command of the Lord.

Therefore, your body will not be buried with the burial of your forefathers. The man of God went on his way; a lion attacked him and killed him.

Some people were passing by; they saw the lion is standing on his corpse on the road.

**"When he was gone, a lion met him on the road and killed him. And his corpse was thrown**

**on the road, and the donkey stood by it. The lion also stood by the corpse."** 1 Kings 13:11-26, NKJV.

### Elijah Declares a Drought:

Elijah from Tishbite in Gilead said to Ahab as the Lord of Israel lives. There will not be dew or nor rain in the land for the next few years except at my word.

**"And Elijah the Tishbite, of the inhabitants of Gilead, said to Ahab. As the Lord God of Israel lives, before whom I stand, there shall not be dew nor rain these years, except at my word."** 1 Kings 17:1, NKJV.

### Elijah Fed by Ravens:

The Word of the Lord came to Elijah said: take off from here. Go to the eastward, east of the Jordan, to hide out by the Brook Cherith, which continues into the Jordan.

I have directed the ravens to deliver food for you that you may eat. Elijah went to the east of the Jordan.

The ravens served him and brought him bread and meat in the morning. The ravens brought bread and meat in the evening again, and he drank water from the brook.

**"So, he went and did according to the word of the Lord, for he went and stayed by the Brook Cherith, which flows into the Jordan. The ravens brought him bread and meat in the morning, and bread and meat in the evening; and he drank from the brook."** 1 Kings 17:2-6, NKJV.

**The Widow Makes Food for Elijah:**

There was a drought in the land, the Word of the Lord came to Elijah, go to Zarephath. You meet a widow, and she will provide food for you.

Elijah met her and asked to bring water for him, also to bring bread. She said: I have a handful of flour and a little oil in a jar. I am preparing some food for myself and my son and then to die.

Elijah said: Do not have fear, prepare the food with your bin of flour, and your oil in the jar will not run out dry.

She went to make food for the man of God and herself and her son. At the time of drought, God provided food for her family, according to the Word of God.

**"So, she went away and did according to the word of Elijah; and she and he and her household ate for many days. The bin of flour was not**

**used up, nor did the jar of oil run dry, according to the word of the Lord which He spoke by Elijah."** 1 Kings 17:14-16, NKJV.

**The Drought Ends:**

There was a drought in the land; there was an expectation for heavy rain will come down soon.

Elijah reached up to the top of Carmel; he kneeled down and put his face between his knees; he prayed for abundant rain.

He spoke to his servant, go and see at sea; is there any cloud coming? His servant came back saying: nothing yet!

His servant went to see about six times, but on the seven-times, the servant went to see any cloud on the way.

The servant came to Elijah; he said: I see a small cloud like a hand of a man rising out of the sea. Elijah said to go to tell Ahab, and there is abundant rain falling.

**"Now it happened in the meantime that the sky became black with clouds and wind, and there was a heavy rain. So, Ahab rode away and went to Jezreel."** 1 Kings 18:41-45, NKJV.

**Elijah's Mount Carmel Victory:**

Ahab sent to all prophets and the prophet Elijah to bring a sacrifice on the Alter on Mount Carmel. There were almost four hundred and fifty men of Baal's prophets.

But Elijah was alone by himself as a prophet of Israel. Baal's prophets started to prepare their Alter with one bull cutting in pieces, woods, but no fire underwoods.

They call the god of Baal to send fire to burn the woods to make a sacrifice offering for them.

No answer, they ask again until noontime and evening, but no response from the god of Baal.

Elijah stood up to prepare the Alter with twelve stones represent the twelve tribes of the sons of Jacob. He put the wood, cutting bull in pieces, pouring four waterpots with water on the Alter.

In the evening at the time of the offering, Elijah prayed that the Lord brings these people's hearts back to Himself. Then the fire of the Lord fell and burnt sacrifice on the Alter.

**"Then the fire of the Lord fell and consumed the burnt sacrifice, and the wood and the stones**

**and the dust, and it licked up the water that was in the trench."** 1 Kings 18:20-38, NKJV.

**Elijah Speed Up before Ahab:**

The drought ends with the word of Elijah after they were waiting to have rain on the land. Elijah said to his servant, go up to Ahab, tell him.

Before heavy rain is coming down, Ahab needs to prepare himself to go to Jezreel. So, Ahab, on the way to Jezreel.

But the hand of the Lord came upon Elijah, made him speed up to rush powerfully to the entrance of Jezreel ahead of Ahab.

**"Then the hand of the Lord came upon Elijah, and he girded up his loins and ran ahead of Ahab to the entrance of Jezreel."** 1 Kings 18:46, NKJV.

**The Floating Ax Head:**

The sons of the prophets said to Elisha, the place we are staying with you is very small. Let's go to Jordan to make a house to dwell on there.

So, they found the place to cut trees, one of the servants' iron ax heads fall into the water. The servant was anxious; he said: it was borrowed.

So, Elisha cut the stick he threw into the water, it made an iron float stayed over water. The servant went into the water, where the iron float was, he put his hand into the water. He took an iron ax head under the water.

**"So, the man of God said, "Where did it fall?" And he showed him the place. So, he cut off a stick, and threw it in there; and he made the iron float. Therefore, he said, "Pick it up for yourself." So, he reached out his hand and took it."** 2 Kings 6:1-7, NKJV.

**Elisha Purifies the Pot of Stew:**

Elisha turned to Gilgal; it was a famine in the land. There was the son of the prophets who came around him, Elisha asked his servant to cook the stew for these men.

One man reached out to the pickup herbs, a wild vine, and wild gourds gathered them from the field.

They cooked and brought to serve these men. They said: Master Elisha, we cannot eat this stew in the pot. They said: we see a death in the pot.

So, Elisha takes some flour, puts it in the pot; he said: nothing is harmful in the pot, eat your stew.

**"So, he said, "Then bring some flour." And he put it into the pot, and said, "Serve it to the people, that they may eat." And there was nothing harmful in the pot."** 2 Kings 4:38-41, NKJV.

**Captains and his Men Consumed by the Fire:**

Ahaziah fell on the lattice of his upper room got injured in Samaria. Ahaziah said, there is no God in Israel.

Therefore, he sent a messenger to Baal-Zebub, the god of Ekron, to help him for getting recover from his injury. The Lord heard it and made a judgment upon Ahaziah.

He sends a Captain of fifty men to meet Elijah; they told Elijah: he needs to come down to meet the king. Elijah said to Captain: if I am a man of God, let the fire of the Lord will consume you and your men.

According to the word of Elijah: The fire of God came down and destroyed them all. Ahaziah sent another captain with fifty men again to Elijah, and then they were consumed by the fire of the Lord again.

Ahaziah sends the third Captain with fifty men to Elijah, and the Captain fell on his knees;

he pleaded for mercy from him and his men not to be consumed by the fire of the Lord.

Then the angel of the Lord appeared there and spoke to Elijah to go with them to meet Ahaziah.

He went to see him; Elijah spoke the word of the Lord to Ahaziah, that he didn't believe that there is a God in Israel; therefore, you indeed die.

**"Then he said to him, "Thus says the Lord: Because you have sent messengers to inquire of Baal-Zebub, the god of Ekron, is it because there is no God in Israel to inquire of His word? Therefore, you shall not come down from the bed to which you have gone up, but you shall surely die." 2 Kings 1:15-17, NKJV.**

**Elijah and Elisha Dividing Water in Jordan:**

Elisha was following Elijah going to Jericho, then going to Jordan together before Elijah is taken up to heaven.

At the place in Jordan, they saw fifty men from afar. Elijah and Elisha stood in front of the water, Elijah took his cloak and struck the water.

The water divided from left to right; they crossed over on the dry ground. Immediately, a chariot of fire and horses of fire came to pick up Elijah, then Elisha took Elijah's garment. Elisha went back and stood in front of the water.

He began to strike the water with Elijah's cloak, and the water divided; he crossed it over on the dry ground.

**"Now Elijah took his mantle, rolled it up, and struck the water; and it was divided this way and that, so that the two of them crossed over on dry ground."** 2 Kings 2:1-14, NKJV.

**Elijah Ascends to Heaven:**

The time came to take up Elijah to heaven. Elijah and Elisha were coming back from Gilgal to Bethel and wanted to cross Jordan.

They stood there, Elijah took his mantle and rolled it up, then struck the water got divided. So, they passed it to dry ground.

Elijah asked Elisha, what can I serve you before I go away from you? Elisha replied, let me have **a double portion of your spirit!** Elijah said you asked a difficult thing!

Suddenly, it happened, a chariot of fire arrived with horses of fire by a whirlwind, Elijah went up into heaven.

**"Then it happened, as they continued on and talked, that suddenly a chariot of fire appeared with horses of fire and separated the two of them; and Elijah went up by a whirlwind into heaven."** 2 Kings 2:10-11, NKJV.

**Water Healed by Elisha:**

The people of the city came to Elisha to explain about the situation of the city is very good. But there are other problems in the city is the water of the city became very bad, and the land is fruitless.

So, Elisha said: bring me the salt, he threw the salt into the water. What the Lord said: I have healed this water.

It will never lead to death or perform the land fruitless again. And the water has continued fresh and pure to this day, according to the word Elisha had spoken.

**"So, the water remains healed to this day, according to the word of Elisha which he spoke."** 2 Kings 2:19-22, NKJV.

**Mocking Elisha by Youth:**

Elisha was walking on the road at Bethel, he met some youths were standing on the road. This forty-two of the teenagers began to mock Elisha, tell him; you Baldhead!

You Baldhead! Elisha stirred at them, and he had a spoke curse on them. Suddenly two female bears showed up out of the woods; they attacked these youths; they were mauled and tore apart by bears.

**"So, he turned around and looked at them, and pronounced a curse on them in the name of the Lord. And two female bears came out of the woods and mauled forty-two of the youths."** 2 Kings 2:23-24, NKJV.

**Elisha Spoke for Water Supplied:**

Jehoshaphat king of Judah, the king of Israel, and the king of Edom were gathering as an alliance to go to war against Moab.

They had a meeting in which direction to attack the enemy, but they said: through the desert of Edom.

They came out to march around the land for seven days. But the area was empty and dry, there was no water for the army and no water for the horses.

They needed guidance and water supplies. They were told by one of the servants that there is a prophet in the land named Elisha.

Three kings went to find him, and they needed Elisha's help. Then Elisha spoke the Word of the Lord; you will see water in the valley. You, and your cattle, your animals will drink water.

The Lord will deliver your enemy Moab in your hand. In the morning, suddenly, the water came to the area of Edom, and the land filled with water.

**"Now it happened in the morning, when the grain offering was offered, that suddenly water came by way of Edom, and the land was filled with water."** 2 Kings 3:16-20, NKJV.

### Feeding of a Hundred:

A man came from Baal Shalishah, he brought twenty loaves of barley bread which has baked already.

Elisha said: give it to these people to eat. Elisha's servant wondered how it could be to feed these men.

They were feeding these hundred men, and they ate their bread with some leftover.

**"So, he set it before them; and they ate and had some left over, according to the word of the Lord."** 2 Kings 4:42-44, NKJV.

**The Blinded Syrians Captured:**

As we learn, the king of Syria was preparing to go to war against Israel. Then Elisha forwarded a message to the King of Israel that does not pass through this place in which the Syrian army was coming down.

The King of Syria set up to come down to surrender the city all night. The next day Elisha's servant went out to see out there. He saw a massive army of Syria around the city.

Elisha's servant said to Elisha, master, what shall we do now? So, Elisha prayed to the Lord that He would blind the eyes of all armies.

The Lord struck the whole army with blindness according to the word of Elisha. They took all army troops with blind eyes to Samaria.

Elisha prayed again; the Lord opens these men's eyes to see. The Lord opened all of the army's eyes, according to the word of Elisha.

All of them received their sight, and they saw themselves that they were in Samaria.

**"So, when the Syrians came down to him, Elisha prayed to the Lord, and said, "Strike this people, I pray, with blindness." And He struck them with blindness according to the word of Elisha."** 2 Kings 6:8-20, NKJV.

**Elisha saw Horses and Chariots of Fire:**

Elisha rose in the early morning there was an army of horses and chariots surrender the city. His servant said: what shall we do now?

Elisha said: do not have a fear, he prayed, he saw the Lord made an unseen army. The Lord brought His army with horses and chariots of fire. They were all around the mountain with full army surrender Elisha.

**"And Elisha prayed, and said, "Lord, I pray, open his eyes that he may see." Then the Lord opened the eyes of the young man, and he saw. And behold, the mountain was full of horses and chariots of fire all around Elisha."** 2 kings 6:15-17, NKJV.

**Shadow Backward Ten Degrees:**

The Lord has spoken to Isaiah to go to inform Hezekiah that the Lord has heard his cry and his prayer. He will heal his sickness and will not die. The Lord extended fifteen years by God's mercy to his life.

**"Hezekiah asked Isaiah; what is the sign that the Lord healed me?"** 2 kings 20:8, NKJV.

Isaiah said: The Lord has promised what He told you to do. He will bring ten degrees of shadow backward.

So, Isaiah, the prophet prayed to the Lord. He made the shadow ten degrees backward, and it had moved down on the sundial of Ahaz.

**"So, Isaiah the prophet cried out to the Lord, and He brought the shadow ten degrees backward, by which it had gone down on the sundial of Ahaz."** 2 kings 20:10-11, NKJV.

**The Plague of Tumors in the City:**

The Ark of God has been taken away by the Philistines from Ebenezer to Ashdod. The Ark of God sent to Gath, the hand of the Lord was against that city.

The people were in panic; He tormented the people of the city with a plague of tumors. The people asked the ruler the Philistines, and we must move the Ark of God to Ekron.

When the people of Ekron knew that the Ark of God is entering their city. All people were in a panic again. They heard in another city how the hand of God brought affliction to the people.

They shouted out with their heart for help. Some people died, and some people did not die, but they got a plague of tumors.

**"And the men who did not die were stricken with the tumors, and the cry of the city went up to heaven."** 1 Samuel 5:10-12, NKJV.

**The Lord Struck the Beth Shemesh:**

After the Ark of the Lord returns to Beth Shemesh, the people offered a trespass offering to God and sacrificed to the Lord.

These five Philistines rulers sent as a guilt offering the gold tumors to the Lord. One each fortified to their land. They set up a large stone; they placed the Ark of the Lord on the rock in the area of Joshua of Beth Shemesh.

These men looked inside the Ark of the Lord. The Lord struck fifty thousand and seventy men died. The people mourned, they said: who can stand in the presence of God.

**"Then He struck the men of Beth Shemesh because they had looked into the ark of the**

**Lord. He struck fifty thousand and seventy men of the people, and the people lamented because the Lord had struck the people with a great slaughter."** 1 Samuel 6:17-20, NKJV.

**Great Supernatural Thunder at Ebenezer:**

Samuel spoke to the house of Israel, saying if you return to the Lord with the whole heart and remove all other gods: the Baals and the Ashtoreths.

The God of Israel will bring your enemy Philistines to you. The people of Israel agreed to do so, Samuel said: gather the people at Mizpah.

The Philistines heard about the people of Israel gathered in Mizpah; they said: we will go against Israel.

The people of Israel heard that the Philistines were coming against them. They asked Samuel to pray and intercede for them that God will protect them. Samuel prayed and cried out with a lamb burnt offering to the Lord for Israel.

The Lord answered the prayer; He sent a rumble of thunder and brought confusion upon the Philistines. The people of Israel overcame them.

They chased the Philistines and drew them back. Samuel put a stone between Mizpah and Shen, and it's called Ebenezer; The Lord has helped us.

**"Now as Samuel was offering up the burnt offering, the Philistines drew near to battle against Israel. But the Lord thundered with a loud thunder upon the Philistines that day, and so confused them that they were overcome before Israel."** 1 Samuel 7:5-12, NKJV.

**Feared of the Lord by Thunder and Rain:**

The people of Israel rebelled against God by following other gods and worshipping the god of the Baals and Ashtoreths.

Samuel warned the people that if they don't leave all other gods and worship the God of Israel only. God has already given them a king over them.

The Lord wants to rule over His people as well. Samuel pointed out again if you fear the Lord, to serve Him, to obey His voice only.

But do not rebel against the commandment of the Lord again. If you do rebel against the Lord, the hand of the Lord will come against you.

Samuel prayed and said: because of your wickedness, you see His great things will happen. Suddenly the Lord sent thunder and rain over people. The people respected Samuel and honor the Lord.

**"So, Samuel called to the Lord, and the Lord sent thunder and rain that day; and all the people greatly feared the Lord and Samuel."** 1 Samuel 12:16-18, NKJV.

**Sound of Trees at Rephaim:**

David asked the Lord if I go to attack the Philistines, and will you turn over them into my hands. The Lord said: I surely deliver the enemy into your hands.

God instructed David; you shall not move straight up. Go around the circle behind them, and you shall attack in front of the balsam trees.

When as soon as you hear the sound of marching in the tops of the mulberry trees. You must act immediately because the Lord has moved out in front of you to attack the Philistine army.

David did what the Lord has commanded him to do the right action to attack the Philistines all the way from Gibeon to Gezer.

**"And it shall be, when you hear the sound of marching in the tops of the mulberry trees, then you shall advance quickly. For then the Lord will go out before you to strike the camp of the Philistines."** 2 Samuel 5:22-25, NKJV.

**The Lord Struck Uzzah:**

David assembled all the thirty thousand men of Israel to bring the ark of God from Baale Judah. So, they placed the ark of God on the cart and carried it from the house of Abinadab, which was on the hillside.

These sons of Abinadab; Uzzah and Ahio were escorting the ark of God on the new cart. David and all the men of Israel were celebrating in front of the Ark of God.

When they reached the threshing floor of Nakon, suddenly, the oxen stumble. Uzzah reached out with his hand to hold the Ark of God, not fall off the cart. The anger of the Lord arose. He struck him; he died there.

**"Then the anger of the Lord was aroused against Uzzah, and God struck him there for his error; and he died there by the ark of God."** 2 Samuel 6:6-7, NKJV.

**The Glory Entered the House:**

After King Solomon dedicated the House of God with prayer, and he sacrificed sheep and oxen. At the end of his prayer, the fire of God came down from heaven consumed the burnt offering and the sacrifices.

All the people began to offer their sacrifices before the Lord. Even the priests couldn't enter the House. The Glory of the Lord came down, filled the House, and the Spirit of the Lord poured out in the House of God.

All the people were standing around the house, and they saw the fire of God. They bow down on their faces, worshipping and praising the God of Israel.

**"When all the children of Israel saw how the fire came down, and the glory of the Lord on the temple, they bowed their faces to the ground on the pavement, and worshiped and praised the Lord, saying: "For He is good, for His mercy endures forever."** 2 Chronicles 7:1-3, NKJV.

**Protection Three Men from Furnace:**

As we read about these three Jewish brave men. Shadrach, Meshach, and Abed-nego did not bow themselves to worship other gods, which King Nebuchadnezzar made a law.

When everyone hears the sound of music, they must bow down and worship the golden image. These three men were working over the tasks of the province of Babylon.

They forwarded a message to the King that these men will not worship the golden image.

He called these men; he asked them why you men will not worship the golden image? They said: we serve our God only.

He will send them into a fiery fire furnace, and they said: our God will deliver us from the fire.

They placed them in the furnace; then, the King looked inside; he said: I see four persons are there, and I see the One who is the Son of God.

The King was brought back from the fiery furnace with no burning in their body. He will praise God of Israel.

**"And the satraps, administrators, governors, and the king's counselors gathered together, and they saw these men on whose bodies the fire had no power; the hair of their head was not singed nor were their garments**

**affected, and the smell of fire was not on them."**
Daniel 3:26-27, NKJV.

**Daniel Rescued in the Lions' Den:**

King Darius's kingdom was over one hundred and twenty satraps in the Medes and Persians. Daniel was serving as a provincial governor.

He had such an excellent spirit; the king trusted him. Other governors were trying to find some faults to charge against him, but they couldn't find any wrongdoing.

They made a plot with an excellent plan to accuse him through his God. They brought an approach to the attention of the king.

They said: if anyone who will worship or pray to other gods within thirty days except to the king, his majesty, that would go against the king and shall be thrown into the lion's den.

The king was pleased and signed it and made a new law. Behind the scenes, they were watching Daniel; how he is praying. They saw Daniel, and he would pray to His God three times a day.

They reported to the king; he ordered Daniel will throw into the lion's den. The king was not happy to see that Daniel is in the lion's den. He left, and he went to his palace, he couldn't rest all night.

The king woke up in the early morning came to see Daniel is still alive or not? He opened the lion's den; he asked: Daniel, are you still there?

Daniel said: I am still here, an angel of the Lord came to shut the mouths of these lions, they have not hurt me, because I have found the innocent in the sight of God and my king Darius.

Then the king took Daniel out of the den. He ordered those governors who were trying to accuse Daniel, and they have thrown with all their families in the lion's den.

**"Now the king was exceedingly glad for him, and commanded that they should take Daniel up out of the den. So, Daniel was taken up out of the den, and no injury whatever was found on him, because he believed in his God."** Daniel 6:21-24, NKJV.

### Jonah Thrown into the Sea Became Peaceful:

As the story of Jonah would tell us. Where they were sailing on the sea, and a storm was raging, which Jonah was on the board.

The crews were wondering, and there is a man who can be here, Jonah acknowledged himself. He told them this is me; the sea is roaring; that's why the ship gets to turn over.

You must throw me into the sea. The moment the crews have thrown Jonah into the sea. The Word said: the sea came to break off from its roaring and became very peaceful.

**"So, they picked up Jonah and threw him into the sea, and the sea ceased from its raging."** Jonah 1:15, NKJV.

## Jonah in the Fish's Belly:

The Lord directed the prophet, Jonah, to go to preach repentance and the salvation of God in Nineveh, the Assyrian capital.

He will warn the people if they do not believe and repentant to God that the judgment of God will come. Jonah didn't want to obey the command of the Lord.

But he tried to slip away from the divine mission. He fled to Joppa another way to take a ship for Tarshish, which was the opposite direction from Nineveh.

God turned over Jonah with an act of revenge, brought a powerful storm to warn the safety of their ship and its crew member.

They found out that there is someone who is on the ship cause of the storm; it was Jonah. They throw Jonah into the water. God assigned a huge fish to devour Jonah.

When the fish swallows him, while he was in the belly of the big fish for three days, he prayed that the Lord helps him and gets him out of belly fish.

The Lord allowed the fish to vomit Jonah out. He will go to Nineveh to proclaim of Salvation of God. He went to the city; the whole city gave the heart to God.

**"Then Jonah prayed to the Lord his God from the fish's belly. And he said: "I cried out to the Lord because of my affliction, and He answered me. "Out of the belly of Sheol I cried, and You heard my voice."** Jonah 2:1-10, NKJV.

### Plant Grows for Jonah then Dies:

We learned about Jonah after he preached a great message of salvation to the city of Nineveh, he got tired; he sat down on the east side of the city.

The Lord saw him, and He prepared a plant for Jonah. So, the plant grows up from the ground to make a shade over him, and it may feel comfortable to get rest.

He rested and waited to see what is happening to the city after he preached. Of course, the Lord has not destroyed the city because the people have repented their sins.

But Jonah was not happy with it. He enjoyed the plant and gave him shade. The next day the Lord brought a worm to make the plant die.

**"And the Lord God prepared a plant and made it come up over Jonah, that it might be shade for his head to deliver him from his misery.**

**So, Jonah was very grateful for the plant. But as morning dawned the next day God prepared a worm, and it so damaged the plant that it withered."** Jonah 4:5-7, NKJV.

• CHAPTER 4 •

# Healings Recorded

THE OLD TESTAMENT DESCRIBES God's spirit to use His divine authority and power to heal every disease and deliver his people from suffering. The love of God to restore His people.

God declared Himself as the Healer. Healing is a part of the major plans of supernatural works of God, which manifests in the divine operations in humankind.

We have experience since the creation of human formation. All humans have wrestled infirmity, illness, suffering, and injustice everywhere in the world.

These are affected by physical, nervous, intellectual, and spiritual. As we know, disease, hardship, and persecution have consistently been a part of human beings, which is challenging.

The Word of God is telling us; the reason for all suffering of a human is a sin. God has created man without sin. It was Adam and Eva who had to choose to fall into sin or not?

But when they made their path of free choice instead of living by God's law. They disobeyed God; they made their decision to go under the curse of sin.

Then curse carried illness and brought all the miseries in life and going through the suffering of life today.

Let's look at how a man failed into sin. When he made his own action instead of living in the direction of God because the man disobeyed God.

Humans will die under their own sinful act, brought in infirmity, and all the calamities and unfairness of this way of life.

Even though the human sources of illness are connected to sin. Some people get involved with demonic activities, which bring in sickness in their bodies.

But we believe healing is God's will, and he desires to heal every area in our bodies. We know healing is the deepest center of God's heart.

He wants to restore every man who is suffering from any illness. It is a part of his nature and his spirit. It is real for Him to renew someone's life to change.

Today suffering of a human is unbearable; we see every human is trying to survive from all kind's troubles, dilemmas and poverty, hunger, and more. Every person will try to pursue happiness in life.

Every human being will live in this world seeking God differently. Every man will find healing through a range of forms. It will both natural, which is human knowledge through a physician, medical assistant, and supernatural. Also, which is the healing of God that will take place in a human body.

Now we are going to see how many healings have been taken place in the Old Testament:

**Healing Sara's Barrenness:**

od has promised to heal Sara's womb to bring a covenant child to fulfill God's plan.

God has spoken to Abraham that he will have a child, Sara heard about God has healed her and bring forth a child in her old age.

God fulfilled the birth of Isaac and the healing miracle of God has done for His Glory.

**"And Abraham called the name of his son who was born to him—whom Sarah bore to him—Isaac."** Genesis 21:1-7, NKJV.

### Rebekah Healed from Childless:

When Isaac found his wife Rebekah, she was barren; she couldn't have any child. Isaac was sixty years old, prayed to the Lord for his wife, and the Lord accepted his petition, then Rebekah his wife conceived.

So, the Lord gave them twins with Jacob and Esau, and it will be two nations shall be born.

**"Now Isaac pleaded with the Lord for his wife, because she was barren; and the Lord granted his plea, and Rebekah his wife conceived."** Genesis 25:21, NKJV.

### Rachel Healed from Barren:

As we know Rachel, the wife of Jacob was barren, she wanted to have children. She looked at her sister Leah; she gave birth to Jacob's sons and a daughter.

I believe Rachel pleaded and prayed to the God of Israel to heal her womb. The Word said: God remembered her; the Almighty God listened to her prayer. The Lord healed her, gave two sons were Joseph and Benjamin.

**"Then, God remembered Rachel, and God listened to her and opened her womb."** Genesis 30:22, NKJV.

**Healing of Abimelek:**

The Word said, Abimelek king of Gerar wanted children, but his wife barren to have a child.

Abraham prayed to the Lord that He would heal Abimelek's wife, and also his female slaves could have children again.

**"So, Abraham prayed to God; and God healed Abimelech, his wife, and his female servants. Then they bore children."** Genesis 20:17, NKJV.

**Moses's Hand got Restored:**

The Lord said to Moses, put your hand into your cloak, he did, then the Lord said to Moses, take your hand out of the cloak.

Because Moses's skin was leprous like snow, he put back his hand into cloak again; he took it out; it restored his hand with the rest of his body.

**"Furthermore, the Lord said to him, "Now put your hand in your bosom." And he put his hand in his bosom, and when he took it out, behold, his hand was leprous, like snow.**

**And He said, "Put your hand in your bosom again." So, he put his hand in his bosom again, and drew it out of his bosom, and behold, it was restored like his other flesh."** Exodus 4:6-7, NKJV.

## Miriam and Aaron oppose Moses:

Miriam and Aaron began to talk against Moses; they were complaining about Moses's wife and why God has called Moses to serve but not us?

The Lord heard about them complaining.

The Lord called three of them in front of the tent of meeting. The Lord told them that Moses is a humble man, and I have chosen him, and he is my servant.

Miriam's skin turned leprous. Moses prayed to heal her; then, the Lord put her for seven days confined outside of camp, then she got healed.

**"And when the cloud departed from above the tabernacle, suddenly Miriam became leprous, as white as snow. Then Aaron turned**

toward Miriam, and there she was, a leper." Numbers 12:1-15, NKJV.

**Make a Fiery Serpent:**

God was showing the people about faith. It is quite impossible to figure out that looking at a bronze statue could heal someone from snakebite.

It's God who instructed them precisely what to do. It reached a step of faith that God designed for all to get restored. The people looked at the bronze serpent to live and to get healed.

**"So, Moses made a bronze serpent, and put it on a pole; and so, it was, if a serpent had bitten anyone, when he looked at the bronze serpent, he lived."** Numbers 21:8-9, NKJV.

**Manoah's Wife Barren and Childless:**

The Israelites did evil against the eyes of the Lord for forty years. So, the Lord wants to deliver the Israelites into the hand of the Philistines.

There was a man called: Manoah, and his wife didn't have any child. His wife was barren.

Finally, the angel of the Lord appeared to his wife, said: you will be pregnant. Do not drink wine or any other fermented drink and do not eat unclean food.

Your son will be a Nazirite, and it shall be no razor come upon his head, he shall be devoted to God from the womb.

God has chosen your son to deliver the Israelites from the Philistines. The birth of Samson will take place by God's time for His people.

**"For behold, you shall conceive and bear a son. And no razor shall come upon his head, for the child shall be a Nazirite to God from the womb; and he shall begin to deliver Israel out of the hand of the Philistines."** Judges 13:1-5, NKJV.

**Hannah Healed from Barrenness:**

Hannah was seeking God for having a child; she intercedes to get God's favor to receive healing. She received healing from barrenness because of intimate prayer.

The Lord has answered her petition to have a child. She dedicates her child to the Lord. Her son Samuel became a servant as a prophet of God.

**"So, it came to pass in the process of time that Hannah conceived and bore a son, and called his name Samuel, saying, "Because I**

**have asked for him from the Lord."** 1 Samuel 1:9-20, NKJV.

**Naaman Healed of Leprosy:**

The Word said that Naaman was captain of the army of the king of Aram. He had leprosy in his body. He heard about the prophet Elisha. He wanted to get in touch with him to get healed from his illness.

He went down with all his attendants to meet Elisha. So, he heard that Naaman came to see him. And Elisha told his servant to tell Naaman to go down to the Jordan river to wash seven times.

You will be cleaned and healed. Naaman went to the river, what the man of God told him to do. The moment he came out of the water, God restored his body and received healing.

**"So, he went down and dipped seven times in the Jordan, according to the saying of the man of God; and his flesh was restored like the flesh of a little child, and he was clean."** 2 kings 5:1-19, NKJV.

**King Jeroboam, his Hand Shriveled:**

As King Jeroboam came to Bethel to make a sacrificial offering on the Alter to the Lord. The

Man of God from Judah came to stand at Alter and spoke the Word.

King Jeroboam thought the word which he heard from the man of God is the judgment word. He stretched out his hand; said: Seize him. Suddenly the King's hand shriveled up. He couldn't pull his hand back.

He pleaded with the man of God to intercede for his healing that God will restore his hand. The man of God prayed and interceded the Lord, and God healed King's hand.

**"So, it came to pass when King Jeroboam heard the saying of the man of God, who cried out against the altar in Bethel, that he stretched out his hand from the altar, saying, "Arrest him!" Then his hand, which he stretched out toward him, withered, so that he could not pull it back to himself."** 1 Kings 13:4-6, NKJV.

**Elijah Raised a Widow's son to Life:**

The son of the widow became very ill and finally stopped breathing. The mother said to Elijah; you came here to remind my sin and to kill my son.

Elijah took her son, and he went to another room. He cried out to the Lord. The Word said: "he stretched himself out on the boy three times." and the Lord heard Elijah's prayer.

He brought the boy's life return back to him again. Then Elijah took the boy to his mother to give her son alive.

**"Then the Lord heard the voice of Elijah; and the soul of the child came back to him, and he revived."** 1 Kings 17:17-24, NKJV.

**Shunammite Barren's Woman:**

The prophet Elisha passed by through the town Shunem. A couple, man, and wife liked the man of God. Any time Elisha passed by through their city, they invited him to stay in their home.

Elisha was very pleased with their hospitality, and he asked them: how can I serve you? Elijah's servant Gehazi said: they don't have any children.

So, Elisha gave a prophecy over the wife that she will get pregnant; she will have a son next year.

**"So, he said, "Call her." When he had called her, she stood in the doorway. Then he said, "About this time next year you shall embrace a son."** 2 Kings 4:8-17, NKJV.

**Elisha brought the Boy's Life Back:**

The Shunammite's woman's son died, she was desperately in need of healing over her son. She found Elisha; she said to the prophet, I will not leave you until to do something for my son.

So, Elisha sent his servant Gehazi to go to a dead boy. He should put Elisha's rod on the face of the boy to live. Gehazi went to the house, and he did what Elisha told him to do.

But there was no sign of new life in the boy's body. Elisha realized, there was no manifestation of healing to resurrect the dead boy.

He came to the boy's death bed; he laid on the boy's body, and the dead boy's body grew warm, suddenly he sneezed seven times, opened his eyes, and came back to life again.

**"He returned and walked back and forth in the house, and again went up and stretched himself out on him; then the child sneezed seven times, and the child opened his eyes."** 2 Kings 4:29-36, NKJV.

**A Dead Man touched Elisha's Bones:**

A man was dead; some Israelites were trying to bury him. But they threw a dead man into Elisha's tomb, and he touched with Elisha's bones, the dead man raised from death to life. The man began to stand up on his feet.

**"So it was, as they were burying a man, that suddenly they spied a band of raiders; and they put the man in the tomb of Elisha; and when the man was let down and touched the bones of Elisha, he revived and stood on his feet."** 2 Kings 13:21, NKJV.

### Hezekiah Healed from Illness:

Hezekiah had an incurable sickness, and he implored the Lord by crying out from his heart for healing. The Lord heard his prayer; He gave the word to Isaiah to go to Hezekiah, that which the Lord added 15 years to his life.

He would get healed and living for more years. Hezekiah received his healing from the Lord.

**"Isaiah said, Take a lump of figs. And they took and laid it on the boil, and he recovered."** 2 Kings 20:7, NKJV.

### Hezekiah's Prayer for Sennacherib's Threat:

The king of Assyria Sennacherib made war against the land and wanted to take over the city of Jerusalem. Hezekiah king of Judah went to pray and ask for help, which the Lord heard his cry.

The Lord has spoken to the prophets Isaiah to declare the word to King Hezekiah. The Lord will not allow the enemy to take over. The Lord will defend the city of Jerusalem for the sake of David God's servant.

It's passed that night; the angel of the Lord appeared in the camp of Assyrian killed one hundred and eighty-five thousand.

**"And it came to pass on a certain night that the angel of the Lord went out, and killed in the camp of the Assyrians one hundred and eighty-five thousand; and when people arose early in the morning, there were the corpses—all dead."** 2 Kings 19:35, NKJV.

**God Gave him Twice:**

Some critics think Job had nine months of suffering severe health issues. It was an unexpecting disaster for his children and possession. He became humble, and he learned how to trust God.

Job prayed for his friends, and he was sick; the Lord has healed him. God has blessed him with double possession, with more children, with livestock, with a long life.

**"And the Lord restored Job's losses when he prayed for his friends. Indeed the Lord gave Job twice as much as he had before."** Job 42:10-17, NKJV.

**God Restored his Understanding:**

God returned Nebuchadnezzar's understanding of his glory. He said: God added excellent majesty to me. He looked to heaven; he blessed God; he praised God.

He declared: God returned my glory, my kingdom, my honor, my health back to me.

**"And at the end of the time I, Nebuchadnezzar, lifted my eyes to heaven, and my understanding returned to me; and I blessed the Most High and praised and honored Him who lives forever."** Daniel 4:34-36, NKJV.

• CHAPTER 5 •

# The Reason for Infirmity

WE DISCOVER THROUGH THESE stories; there is evidence of the relationship between sin and disease. From the beginning of creation, until our present time, there will be sins that can affect suffering in every life.

As sin does always shows these crises for us. We look at these stories, and then we recognize sin creates more misery for every human being. Now the question can be asked; where are these crises coming from?

From prideful of man, rebellious, disobedient to God, the hardness of heart, sinful greed, not following the law of God.

Surely, God's reaction to sin was committed by his people or by any man for breaking

His rules. But not all diseases resulted through transgression and was not substantial suffering for breaking his laws.

There are privileges to this guideline. Job is a symbol of someone who struggled with sickness with no associated sin or fault.

God justified him, and He brought respect and admired Job. God also reduced sources, caused the land too desolate, or sent enemies to strike and to discipline his people.

Sometimes they brought suffering from a secret sin and carried on with past circumstances. Every man recognizes his sins and will repent to God.

Then the Lord removes all sickness and punishments of the people from their lives. Pharaoh's entire house was exposed to severe plagues because he had been interested to choose Abraham's wife for his palace.

**"But the Lord plagued Pharaoh and his house with great plagues because of Sarai, Abram's wife."** Genesis 12:17, NKJV.

We will look at a few stories, how sins will cause infirmity to every man's life:

The angels of the Lord struck the men who were intimidating Lot's household; they made them blind.

**"And they struck the men who were at the doorway of the house with blindness, both small and great, so that they became weary trying to find the door."** Genesis 19:11, NKJV.

Abraham and Sarah came to the land of Gerar, and he met the king of Gerar. Abraham introduced his wife Sarah as his sister to the King Abimelech of Gerar.

Abimelech was very interested in Sarah, and he took Sarah as his wife.

The Lord came to him in the dream, that **"what you did was wrong,"** you made the man's wife for yourself, do not near to Sarah if you touch her you surely die.

The next morning, he called Abraham, telling him what you have done to me, take your wife. The Lord made all Abimelech's household barren because he unintentionally planned to pick Sarah as his wife.

**"for the Lord had closed up all the wombs of the house of Abimelech because of Sarah, Abraham's wife."** Genesis 20:18, NKJV.

Miriam made false and damaging statements about her brother Moses; she became leprous.

**"Then Aaron turned toward Miriam, and there she was, a leper."** Numbers 12:10, NKJV.

When the Israelites were trying to enter the Promised Land with Moses. Some of them decided to go into idolatry and worship another god Baal Peor.

As we know, the Moabites worshipped the idol Baal Peor as their god, and they were in the territory of Peor. They had a ritual service specifically on sexual performances.

They found Baal's ceremony is related to sexuality and adultery in the temple. They even celebrated him as a pregnancy god who produced children.

Because of their sin, God judged the children of Israel. The Lord saw what happened to his people, which they were worshiping other gods.

The rage of the Lord was stirred up against Israel. He sent the plague to those who died were twenty-four thousand.

**"And those who died in the plague were twenty-four thousand."** Numbers 25:9, NKJV.

The Lord said to Moses, my people have rejected me. How long will they take to believe in me with all the signs and wonders that I have done for them?

The Lord told him that He is sending pestilence to teach them to become a great nation.

**"Then the Lord said to Moses: "How long will these people reject Me? And how long will they not believe Me, with all the signs which I have performed among them?"** Numbers 14:11-12, NKJV.

After the Philistines captured the ark of the Lord for seven months. The plague was sent by the Lord with sickness. Wherever the Ark got seized, the people suffered from tumors.

The people of the Philistines could keep the Ark no longer in the land. So, the leaders had a meeting to send back the Ark of the Lord.

**"So, they said, if you send away the ark of the God of Israel, do not send it empty; but by all means return it to Him with a trespass offering. Then you will be healed, and it will be known to you why His hand is not removed from you."** 1 Samuel 6:1-12, NKJV.

The Lord struck the people who were trying to look into the Ark of the Lord at Beth Shemesh. The Lord was displeased with them.

He struck them with fifty thousand and seventy men and the people who have died with a vast massacre.

**"Then He struck the men of Beth Shemesh, because they had looked into the ark of the Lord. He struck fifty thousand and seventy men of the people, and the people lamented because the Lord had struck the people with a great slaughter."** 1 Samuel 6:19, NKJV.

Because David recorded a census of the people, God was displeased with him, and He wanted to strike Israel.

But the Lord gave three choices to David, So, these choices were: **famine, invasion, and plague** were given to choose.

David recognized his mistake, and he accepted the plague, and the Lord struck seventy thousand people who perished in Israel.

**"So, the Lord sent a plague upon Israel from the morning till the appointed time. From Dan to Beersheba seventy thousand men of the people died."** 2 Samuel 24:15, NKJV.

King Jehoram did evil in the eyes of the Lord. The plague struck down to Jehoram's family, his children, wives, and all properties. The Lord sent a deadly sickness of the bowels.

**"behold, the Lord will strike your people with a serious affliction—your children, your wives, and all your possessions; and you will become very sick with a disease of your intestines, until your intestines come out by reason of the sickness, day by day."** 2 Chronicles 21:14-15, NKJV.

King Uzziah reigned, and he became authoritative, his pride started to his destruction. He was very unfaithful unto the Lord; he went to the temple with a censer in his hand to burn incense.

The priests told him, you will not be allowed to enter the temple, is only the priests can come into the temple. He got angry, while he was threatening the priests unrespectfully.

The Lord saw it, and He smites him with leprosy on his forehead. So, he was living in a separate house until he died because of his pride.

**"And Azariah the chief priest and all the priests looked at him, and there, on his forehead, he was leprous; so they thrust him out of**

**that place. Indeed, he also hurried to get out, because the Lord had struck him."** 2 Chronicles 26:16-20, NKJV.

Sennacherib, King Assyria, his army, was trying to attack Jerusalem. King Hezekiah and the prophet Isaiah were crying out to the Lord in prayer for help.

The Lord sent an angel to strike down the camp of the Assyrian king by night. The angel wiped out all the fighting men and the captains and officers.

He reached into the temple of their god, kill them all with the sword.

**"Then the Lord sent an angel who cut down every mighty man of valor, leader, and captain in the camp of the king of Assyria. So, he returned shamefaced to his own land.**

**And when he had gone into the temple of his god, some of his own offspring struck him down with the sword there."** 2 Chronicles 32:20-21, NKJV.

There was a man who had a high authority as a commander of the army of the king of Aram named Naaman. He had leprosy. He heard there is a prophet in Israel.

He was very interested in going and meeting him to get healed by him. He went to the prophet Elisha; he said to Naaman to wash in the Jordan seven times.

He was upset, even he didn't want to do what Elisha told him to do. His servant encouraged him to go down underwater.

He humbled himself, came out of the water; he got cured. He went to the house of Elisha, giving him gifts that he did for him. Elisha didn't accept his gifts. Meanwhile, they were on their way back home.

But Gehazi stopped them on the road to get their gifts for himself. Gehazi came back to Elisha, and he asks Gehazi; where have you been? So, Gehazi received leprosy's Naaman on himself because of his greedy spirit.

**"Therefore, the leprosy of Naaman shall cling to you and your descendants forever." And he went out from his presence leprous, as white as snow."** 2 Kings 5:26-27, NKJV.

Ahaziah got sick, and he did not want to receive a piece of advice from the God of Israel. The Lord sent the prophet Elijah to him to give a message from God.

Because he asked Baal-Zebub, he didn't want to get healed from God. The Lord said, because you have done this action, you will stay on your bed, and you indeed die.

**"Then he said to him, "Thus says the Lord: Because you have sent messengers to inquire of Baal-Zebub, the god of Ekron, is it because there is no God in Israel to inquire of His word? Therefore, you shall not come down from the bed to which you have gone up, but you shall surely die."** 2 Kings 1:16, NKJV.

As the Philistines captured the ark of God, they carried the ark from Ebenezer to Ashdod. They brought the ark of God into the house of Dagon, which was the place of idol worship.

The next day they came to the house of Dagon. They looked at the Dagon idol fallen on its face on the ground before the ark of the Lord. Cut off the head, and hands, only his body remained.

They set it up, Dagon back to the place. So, they came back the next day they saw the Dagon has fallen on his face before the ark of God again. They asked that no priests of Dagon entered the house of Dagon.

The Lord struck the people of Ashdod and its neighborhood. He carried desolation for them and plagued them with tumors.

**"But the hand of the Lord was heavy on the people of Ashdod, and He ravaged them and struck them with tumors, both Ashdod and its territory."** 1 Samuel 5:1-6, NKJV.

King Asa was the king of the Kingdom of Judah, and he reigned for forty-one years. The Word said: king Asa was a good king and did right in the sight of God.

But in the thirty-ninth year of his reign. He had a disease in his feet very severe. The Word of God said: He got help only from the physicians, but he didn't seek God's healing for his feet.

**"And in the thirty-ninth year of his reign, Asa became diseased in his feet, and his malady was severe; yet in his disease he did not seek the Lord, but the physicians."** 2 Chronicles 16:12, NKJV.

• CHAPTER 6 •

# Miracles in the New Testament

JESUS' MIRACLE HAD RECORDED as a manifestation of the grace and the mercy of God. The Gospels describe the powerful love of God, and it has been released from heaven through His Son Jesus.

The Lord Jesus has accomplished such phenomena by the anointing of God. He is still serving us by His miracles and healing today. He is the Son of God, was anointed with the Holy Spirit.

He performed mighty works of God through God's passion in the Gospels. All crowds were coming from every city to walk forward to receive the bread of life from Jesus. He gives them miracles and healing with grace and forgiving their sins.

In the four books of the Gospels, we see the authors considered these books to show their flocks that Jesus can do miracles and healing today.

There is no power in man's ability to perform miracles as Jesus accomplished by the supernatural hand of God. Only Jesus gave authority to every believer to be able to love, serve, and minister to His people.

Jesus showed His miracles to reveal God's Glory, and He taught us how to have a forgiving heart and to be kind toward others.

God uses these miracles and healing to reveal the Glory of God to the whole world. Sometimes many people must see these demonstrations of God's supreme authority in the world.

It will bring an understanding to some people that there is a God in heaven who performs miracles. Today people are trying to find God in their way.

So, because of their unbelief, these miracles can happen from God to inspire the people as they can trust God by faith.

They believe that there is a Savior; He has done wonders and healing in the New Testament. He can do now among us again.

These extraordinary performing events that Jesus has done in the New Testament. As Jesus repeatedly mentioned, these are signified entirely of his Father's commission.

He will obey to do the will of God. God will honor those who follow His will; Jesus did what the Father has appointed Him to do with mighty miracles in His name.

We see Jesus had power over all demons and casting out unclean spirits.

Jesus performed many miracles, providing food for the multitudes, even nature obeys the command of Him to calm storms.

Jesus had a high authority over the dead to resurrect and bringing back to life.

We will be looking at Jesus' miracles in many different stories in the New Testament. It will give us an understanding of how Jesus has revealed God's power and His authority over sins, natural events, nature, and the work of the devil.

**Jesus Left Invisible Among the Multitude:**

Jesus entered the synagogue; it was a Sabbath day. It was a custom to read scripture; He opened the book of Isaiah, Chapter 61:1-2.

After he read the verse, He said to the people in the synagogue. This scripture has fulfilled in your hearing. The people did not believe Him.

They have all filled with wrath, standing up with anger toward Jesus. Because the people were waiting for the Messiah to come to save them, they rejected Jesus at His town, Nazareth.

They brought Jesus outside the synagogue to throw Him out over the cliff. But He passed through the crowd, and He went on his way.

**"and rose up and thrust Him out of the city; and they led Him to the brow of the hill on which their city was built, that they might throw Him down over the cliff. Then passing through the midst of them, He went His way."** Luke 4:28-30, NKJV.

**Turned Water into Wine:**

There was a wedding in Cana of Galilee. The mother of Jesus arrived, then they invited Jesus along with His disciples; they all came to the wedding.

The host was serving wine to all guests; they had noticed that they ran out of wine for visitors. So, the mother of Jesus came to Him, asking Him, please do something here; they are running out of wine.

Jesus instructed them to fill up the six waterpots with water. They marveled, what is going on here?

Then Jesus told them to take some wines to serve their guests. They served the wines; in fact, the master of the feast said: this is the best wines I have never tested before.

**"When the master of the feast had tasted the water that was made wine, and did not know where it came from (but the servants who had drawn the water knew), the master of the feast called the bridegroom." John 2:1-11, NKJV.**

**Fisherman Became a Fisher of Men:**

Jesus got near to the lake of Gennesaret, the people asked Him to teach the Word of God. Then He saw Peter along with James and John in their boat, and they were washing their nets in the boat.

Jesus asked them to move their boat in the middle of the lake to catch some fishes. They said: Master, we have tried all night we didn't find anything.

If You said so, we would do it when they obeyed the Word of Jesus, after they caught multitudes of fishes. They couldn't believe it, catching many fishes.

They asked other fishermen partners to come to help them. They filled up their boat with many fishes; they began to sink. When Peter saw this miracle happened, he kneeled before Jesus.

He said to Jesus: I am a sinful man. Jesus replied: You will be a fisher of man. These fishermen brought all fishes to the shore; they left everything, and then they followed Jesus.

**"And Jesus said to Simon, "Do not be afraid. From now on you will catch men."** Luke 5:1-11, NKJV.

**Storm Obeys Jesus:**

They left the multitude of people, and they followed Jesus; it becomes evening. Jesus said: let's cross the other side of the water.

Jesus was in the boat, and He went to sleep. A great windstorm arose, and the waves hit the boat so that there was water filling up the boat. They went to Jesus; they woke him up.

They said: Teacher; we are perishing; you don't care about us. Jesus stood up, and He rebuked the storm. It became calm, and peace came to the water and wave.

Jesus said: why are you so afraid, how come that you don't have any faith? These men looked at each other; even storm and wave obey Him?

**"Then He arose and rebuked the wind, and said to the sea, "Peace, be still!" And the wind ceased and there was a great calm."** Mark 4:35-41, NKJV.

**Two Demon-Possessed Men Turned Loosed:**

Jesus had come to the country of the Gergesenes, two demon-possessed men were going out of the tombs; they were extremely dangerous.

They were so powerful that no one could cross that way. They saw Jesus; they said: have you come to torment us Jesus the Son of God? What have we done with you?

When Jesus saw these two men, He looked at the sea, and He saw, there were many swine feeding. These two demon-possessed men asked Jesus to be cast out into many swine!

Jesus commanded to go: all demons came out of these two men into a large swine. These pigs ran violently down into the sea; they perished in the water.

These two men got set free, went to tell the people in their town, the whole city came to meet Jesus.

**"So, the demons begged Him, saying, if You cast us out, permit us to go away into the herd of swine."** Matthew 8:28-34, NKJV.

**Feeding Five Thousand:**

When Jesus heard that John Baptist beheaded in prison, he went by boat to a quiet place to be alone with the Father.

The people heard about Jesus that they wanted to hear from Him; the people walked from cities to find Him.

Jesus came out, and He saw a multitude of people waited on Him. He had great compassion for them. He taught the Word; He healed many sick people.

Then the disciples of Jesus came to Him. They said: we are in an empty place; it is now getting late evening. We need to send people away to their cities and villages to find something to eat.

Jesus answered to His disciples: you do not send them away; you can feed them. The disciples said to Him: we have only five loaves and two fish.

Then Jesus took up the five loaves and two fish to heaven. He blessed it and broke the loaves and fish.

He gave it to His disciples to serve the people; they were five thousand men, besides women and children ate. They were eating, and the leftover of the food-filled up on the baskets remained.

**"Now those who had eaten were about five thousand men, besides women and children."** Matthew 14:13-21, NKJV.

### Jesus Walked on the Water:

Jesus served His disciples to go into the boat, and they left before Him to the other side. He sent the crowd of people away.

He continued to serve the people; He left there, to go up the mountain to be in the presence of His Father to pray.

He knew there would be a storm in the evening. The storm brings the waves, and a strong wind hits the sea. The disciples of Jesus were in the boat in the middle of the sea.

I believe Jesus went to rescue them. Suddenly the disciples saw someone afar who is walking on water, they were all scared, they said: it is a ghost! Jesus said to them: **"This is I"** do not have fear.

Peter said: Lord if it is You, let me come to you and Peter wants to walk on water. Jesus allows him to come.

Peter went out of the boat, but he feeds on the water. He looked down, and he was afraid. He went down into the water; he said: save me, Lord.

Jesus reached out His hand and took him out of the water. Jesus said, why did you have a doubt and have no faith?

The wind got quiet. Those who were in the boat saw everything that happened; they worshipped Him, saying, you are the Son of God.

**"Now in the fourth watch of the night Jesus went to them, walking on the sea."** Matthew 14:22-33, NKJV.

**Jesus Fed Four Thousand:**

They followed Jesus to listen to Him, learning about the Kingdom of God. The people followed him for three days; they were hungry.

Jesus said: I have great compassion for these people. I cannot send them away to their city and home because some people came from a long distance.

He said to His disciples: how many loaves do you have? They answered: seven. Jesus said, let them sit down on the ground. He took the seven loaves, blessed it, and He broke it.

Then He gave it to His disciples to serve the people who were waiting to eat. The people ate their food, and they picked up seven full baskets of leftovers. The multitude were about four thousand people.

**"So, they ate and were filled, and they took up seven large baskets of leftover fragments. Now those who had eaten were about four thousand. And He sent them away."** Mark 8:1-9, NKJV.

**Coin Inside the Mouth of Fish:**

The disciples came to Capernaum, and those people from tax collectors came to Peter asked them: does your Teacher pay tax? He said: Yes.

Then Jesus arrived there, and He heard they were asking Peter to pay tax. Jesus responded to Peter. Do you expect the kings of the earth will collect taxes from their children or others?

Peter answered: From others. Jesus said: Peter, go to the sea, throw your fishing line, cast your hook, and catch a fish, open the mouth of fish. You will find a coin, take it, pay my taxes and yours.

**"Nevertheless, lest we offend them, go to the sea, cast in a hook, and take the fish that comes up first. And when you have opened its mouth, you will find a piece of money; take that and give it to them for Me and you."** Matthew 17:24-27, NKJV.

**The Fig Tree Dried:**

Jesus with His disciples returned to the city near Bethany, and He was hungry. They all were passing by the fig tree.

Jesus saw a fig tree and came near to the tree; he noticed, there are leaves up, but they can find nothing on the tree.

Jesus said to the tree: Let no one eat your fruit again! Immediately the fig tree dried. His disciples heard what Jesus said.

**"In response Jesus said to it, "Let no one eat fruit from you ever again." And His disciples heard it."** Mark 11:12-14, NKJV.

**Healing the Ear of Servant of the High Priest:**

Now the time came to arrest Jesus in Gethsemane, all of the servants of the high priest were surrounding Jesus.

Judas was there with them, he came to Jesus, and He said to Judas, have you betrayed the Son of Man with a kiss?

They were trying to arrest Him, one of the disciples struck the servant of the high priest with the sword, and he cut off his ear.

Jesus said: permit me before we go. He touched the servant of the high priest's ear healed him there.

**"And one of them struck the servant of the high priest and cut off his right ear. But Jesus answered and said, "Permit even this." And He**

**touched his ear and healed him."** Luke 22:49-51, NKJV.

**Breakfast by the Sea of Tiberias:**

Jesus's disciples were together; Simon Peter, Thomas, Nathanael, the sons of Zebedee, and two other disciples.

Jesus revealed Himself to them at the sea of Tiberias. Peter told them: I am going fishing! Others responded we are coming with you.

They went into their boat, cast their nets, tried all night they caught nothing until the next day. In the morning, Jesus appeared to them on the shore.

They didn't recognize Jesus; He asked them: have you had any food yet? No? Jesus said: cast your nets on the right side; you will catch some fishes there.

They did; they caught many fishes to help each other to drag nets out with a multitude of fishes to the shore. They saw Jesus made a fire of coals, which put bread and fishes on it to cook.

Jesus asked them to bring fishes that caught them. They caught one hundred and fifty-three fishes. Jesus invited them to eat breakfast after hard work.

Jesus served them and how Jesus revealed himself for the third time to His disciples after His resurrection.

**"Jesus said to them, "Come and eat breakfast." Yet none of the disciples dared ask Him, "Who are You?"—knowing that it was the Lord. Jesus then came and took the bread and gave it to them, and likewise the fish."** John 21:1-14, NKJV.

# Miracles Resurrection

**Jesus Raises the Son of the Widow:**
JESUS WENT TO A city called Nain along with His disciples. When He came near to the town gate. He saw a large crowd, and they carried out with a coffin with a dead young man who was the son of a widow.

Jesus said to the widow; do not weep, Jesus touched the coffin. He saw a dead man lying down. He said: arise a young man, I say to you.

The dead man moved and began to speak. Jesus presented the alive man to his mother. The news went all around the city that there is a prophet among us; God has visited us.

The people were praising God for miracles. The miracle report has gone throughout Judea and all regions.

**"Then He came and touched the open coffin, and those who carried him stood still. And He said, "Young man, I say to you, arise." So, he who was dead sat up and began to speak. And He presented him to his mother."** Luke 7:11-17, NKJV.

**Raising Death, the Daughter of Jairus:**

Jesus had crossed over by boat to the other side. A great multitude gathered around Him, one of the rulers his name Jairus from the synagogue approached Him.

He fell at the feet of Jesus; he said: my daughter is very sick; she is at the point of death. Would you come to heal my daughter that she will live again? He went with him to his house.

Also, Jesus healed many on His way. While He was going to Jairus's house, someone came to him said: your daughter is dead; there is no need to come. Jesus said: belief only, she is sleeping.

He allowed Peter, James, and John the brother of James to go with Him. He reached the house of Jairus, a disturbance, and those who mourned and wept loudly.

He said to them, **"Why are you making this confusion and grieve?"** Your daughter is not dead. They mocked Him; He ordered the father and the mother of the child, and others who came with Him will come into the room.

He took the hand of a child, said: **"I say to you a little girl, arise."** Instantly the girl arose and stood on her feet, she walked.

He told the parents to give the child food to eat, and they were all amazed by the miracle resurrection from the dead to life.

**"Then He took the child by the hand, and said to her, "Talitha, cumi," which is translated, "Little girl, I say to you, arise." Immediately the girl arose and walked, for she was twelve years of age. And they were overcome with great amazement."** Mark 5:41-42, NKJV.

**Lazarus Resurrected from the Dead:**

There was a man from Bethany, his name; Lazarus was very sick. Mary and Martha were very concerned about their brother. These two sisters sent a message to Jesus that Lazarus is very ill.

He said, this sickness is not to death but brings Glory to God and glorified the Son of God. Jesus stayed for two days. He didn't go to Lazarus.

After He said to His disciples, let's go to Judea. Our friend Lazarus is sleeping; I may need to wake him up.

Jesus said to his disciples that Lazarus is dead; I am glad I was not there; now, you may believe more. Jesus went there, and He found out that he already dead for four days.

Many people with Mary and Martha were mourning the death of Lazarus. Jesus was approaching the town. Martha heard that Jesus is coming; she went to meet him.

Martha said: Lord; if you were here, my brother did not die. Jesus said to her: I assure you he will rise again. Where did you lay Lazarus?

Jesus met Mary at the tomb; she fell and said if you were here, my brother did not die. They opened the tomb, Jesus said: you just believe, you would see the Glory of God.

Jesus prayed to the Father, He said: you have heard me, and you hear me in front of these people that you have sent me.

Then Jesus called with a loud voice, **Lazarus, come forth!** Suddenly, dead Lazarus came out of the tomb, **walking with a cloth.** Jesus said: lose him, let him go.

**"Now when He had said these things, He cried with a loud voice, "Lazarus, come forth!" And he who had died came out bound hand and foot with graveclothes, and his face was wrapped with a cloth. Jesus said to them, "Loose him, and let him go." John 11:1-44, NKJV.**

• CHAPTER 8 •

# Healing of Jesus

Supernatural healing is the action of God through Jesus, who brings new life into every man's destiny. We see Jesus in the New Testament.

He was and is the anointed One to perform healing in the body of a non-believer and a believer. Jesus had love and compassion for lost souls and sick people.

Jesus has delivered many people from spiritual suffering. Many had emotional and mental problems; Jesus acknowledged it to set them free.

Healing was in Jesus's heart and is still there to touch His people to restore them in His name only.

The Lord uses every Christian believer to anoint the sick person with the anointing of Oil. They will receive healing by faith.

Jesus's anointing touched the sick and healed them because he had sympathy for many who suffered in pain of illness.

But even better indeed, as He did with all His wonders, he finished the plan of God. The Father was reaching the plan of Salvation through him.

He declared that He accomplished by the Father's purpose to send Him into the world to find the lost souls.

Jesus was passing through all the villages and cities. He was preaching and teaching the Word of God in the synagogues, and declaring the Good News of the kingdom. He had a love of the Father to heal every infirmity.

There will be the expression of the triumph of King Jesus and His reign. The healing of Jesus is the demonstration of His greatness and authority.

We will look at many beautiful stories of the healing of Jesus in His early ministry. He was walking among the people who were suffering from sickness and death.

He had such a great love for the people, and He is still healing His people who have faith and believe in His Word.

**Two Blind Men Healed:**

After Jesus departed the house of Jairus, He healed his daughter. He was on the way back, two blinded men followed Him.

They said to Jesus: Son of David, have mercy on us! Jesus appeared to them and asked, do you believe?

That I can be able to do this for you? They answered: Yes, Lord. Jesus touched their eyes, saying because you believed now you are healed.

They received their sight, rejoicing and spreading the good news to the whole town.

**"Then He touched their eyes, saying, "According to your faith let it be to you." And their eyes were opened."** Matthew 9:27-31, NKJV.

**A Dumb Demon-possessed Healed:**

When Jesus went His way, they brought a man who was a dumb demon-possessed. Jesus cast out every devils and demon out of his life.

He got healed to speak, thinking perfectly and getting right with God. People were watching, and they marveled that there was never like this happening in Israel.

**"As they went out, behold, they brought to Him a man, mute and demon-possessed. And when the demon was cast out, the mute spoke. And the multitudes marveled, saying, "It was never seen like this in Israel!"** Matthew 9:30-33, NKJV.

**Jesus Heals the Deaf and Dumb:**

Jesus left the region of Tyre and Sidon. He came near the area of the part of Decapolis to the Sea of Galilee. The people were expecting to see Jesus.

They brought a man who had deaf and a hindrance in his speech. They begged Him to heal this man. Jesus placed His fingers into his ears, He spits, and He touched the man's tongue.

Jesus looked into heaven, **"Be opened."** Immediately, the man felt that his ears opened, his tongue loosed, and he started to speak.

The people were there watching the healing miracles of Jesus, and they overwhelmed with astonishment. They said: He has done the marvelous things in our midst.

**"And He took him aside from the multitude, and put His fingers in his ears, and He spat and touched his tongue.**

**Then, looking up to heaven, He sighed, and said to him, "Ephphatha," that is, "Be opened."**

**Immediately his ears were opened, and the impediment of his tongue was loosed, and he spoke plainly."** Mark 7:31-37, NKJV.

**A Blind Man Healed at Bethsaida:**

Jesus came to Bethsaida, and the people were around him and brought a blind man to Jesus to heal his sight. They begged him; Jesus touched his eyes to receive his sight.

He took him out of that area, then Jesus made a spit, touched his eyes. He asked, can he see anything? He said: I see men as trees, walking around.

Jesus put His hands on his eyes one more time. He restored a new sight to his eyes. He got healed, and he could see clearly. He sent him away not to tell anyone in his town.

**"And when He had spit on his eyes and put His hands on him, He asked him if he saw anything. And he looked up and said, "I see men like trees, walking." Then He put His hands on**

**his eyes again and made him look up. And he was restored and saw everyone clearly."** Mark 8:22-26, NKJV.

**Healed a Woman with A Spirit of Infirmity:**

Jesus was in the synagogues and teaching on the Sabbath. He saw a woman bound by the spirit of infirmity for eighteen years.

When she bent over, and she could not lift herself at all. Jesus said to her: Woman, you are set free from your infirmity now.

When the moment He ministered to her by laying hands on her. The woman received her healing in her body, and she got straight up; she started to glorify God.

**"But when Jesus saw her, He called her to Him and said to her, "Woman, you are loosed from your infirmity." And He laid His hands on her, and immediately she was made straight, and glorified God."** Luke 13:10-13, NKJV.

**Dropsy Man Healed on the Sabbath:**

Jesus entered the house of the Pharisees; there was one of the rulers. When people saw that Jesus was sitting and eating bread on the Sabbath, they brought a man who had dropsy to heal him.

Those Pharisees tried to test Jesus not to heal any man on the Sabbath. But Jesus had compassion for the sick people, and he took him; He healed him, let him go.

**"But they kept silent. And He took him and healed him, and let him go."** Luke 14:1-4, NKJV.

**Ten Lepers Healed:**

As Jesus was coming to Jerusalem and passing by through Samaria and Galilee. He was approaching a certain village He saw ten lepers.

They stood afar from Jesus; they shouted with a loud voice, Jesus, have mercy on us! Jesus said to them: go to the town and show yourself to the priest.

They turned around, and they believed what Jesus told them to do. While they were walking and going back on their way to their villages, all ten lepers got cleansed.

One of the lepers returned and found Jesus; he fell at Jesus's feet to thank Him. What Jesus did for him; he glorified God for his healing.

Jesus said: What happened to the other nine lepers, they got also healed, but they didn't come back to glorify God.

**"So, when He saw them, He said to them, "Go, show yourselves to the priests." And so, it was that as they went, they were cleansed."** Luke 17:11-19, NKJV.

### A Nobleman's Son Healed:

Jesus came back to Cana of Galilee, where He had changed the water into wine. A Nobleman heard about Jesus that He is on the way to Galilee.

He rushed to find Him and meet with Him. He asked Jesus to come down to heal his son is very sick; he is at the point of death.

Jesus said: the people wanted to see signs and wonders than to believe! The Nobleman man said to Jesus: please come down to heal my son.

He said to the Nobleman man: **"Your son lives."** The Nobleman man believed in Jesus's Word. He went on his way back home, and his servants met him on the road.

He gave him the good news: your son is alive. The Nobleman man realized the Word of Jesus is full of truth.

His son got healed, so he remembered the hour and the time Jesus told him. At the same hour, Jesus said the Word of healing over his son. The household of a Nobleman believed in God.

**"So, the father knew that it was at the same hour in which Jesus said to him, "Your son lives." And he himself believed, and his whole household."** John 4:46-54, NKJV.

**A Man Healed at Pool:**

When Jesus went up to Jerusalem, there was the time for celebrating the feast of the Jews. While Jesus was attending the feast in Jerusalem, he saw the sheep market, **a pool called: Bethesda.**

Five porches surround it. There were many sick people laid down at the pool from all kinds of sickness and different infirmities.

At a specific time, an angel goes down and touches the water. After the angel stirred the water for anyone who first jumps into the water gets healed.

Jesus walked around the pool and looked at a man who has been sick for thirty-eight years.

He asked him, do you wish to get well? He said: Anytime an angel stirs up the water in the pool, I wanted to jump in, but someone else goes down into the water before me.

Jesus said to him, get up and take your bed and walk. He stood up, got healed, and walked with praising God on the Sabbath day.

**"Jesus said to him, "Rise, take up your bed and walk." And immediately the man was made well, took up his bed, and walked."** John 5:1-9, NKJV.

**A Man Born Blind Healed:**

Jesus passed by; He saw a blind man who was born with unseeing eyes. His disciples asked Him: Did he sinned, nor his parents sinned because he was born blind.

Jesus answered: There are none of his parents or himself sinned against God, but it should reveal the Glory of God. He went to the blind man.

He spat and made clay with the saliva. He put on his eyes. He told him, wash your eyes in the pool of Siloam. He washed his eyes; he could see clearly.

The surrounding people watched him. They knew him for a long time because he sat down, begging people for money. People asked, how did he do it?

The blind man said, a man called Jesus. He anointed my eyes. He told me to go to wash it. Now I see it. Jesus is the light of the world; he who believes in Him receives a new life.

**"He answered and said, "A Man called Jesus made clay and anointed my eyes and said to me, 'Go to the pool of Siloam and wash.' So, I went and washed, and I received sight."** John 9:1-12, NKJV.

**A Demon-possessed Daughter Healed:**

Jesus on the way back from the region of Tyre and Sidon. There was a woman of Canaan who came near to Jesus. She cried out and said: have mercy on me, my daughter is demon-possessed!

Jesus didn't respond to her request, and His disciples said: send her away. She kept coming back to approach Him; she worshipped Jesus. She said: help me; Lord.

Jesus said: It will not be a good thing to take the bread to throw it to the dogs. She said: even the dogs will have the crumbs will fall off from their master's tables as well.

Jesus answered, What great faith! He said: **according to your faith**, it will be made healing to your daughter. Her daughter received the healing that at the same hour, Jesus spoke the word to her.

**"Then Jesus answered and said to her, "O woman, great is your faith! Let it be to you as you desire." And her daughter was healed from that very hour."** Matthew 15:21-28, NKJV.

**A Centurion's Servant Healed:**

When Jesus went to Capernaum, a centurion man came to Him. He was pleading to Jesus that his servant is lying at home is very sick. He asked Jesus to come to his house to heal his servant.

Jesus said: **"I will come and heal him."** Matthew 8:7, NKJV.

A centurion man said: Lord, you just speak the word, I believe my servant will get healed. I am not worthy; you would come under my roof. A centurion man continues saying: Lord.

I am a man of authority; I tell my soldiers to do it, he will do, and whatever I asked, he will obey my word.

Jesus was amazed to hear from a centurion man. He said: I have not found such faith in Israel. He said to the centurion man, and you believed it, according to your faith, your servant will get healed.

**"Then Jesus said to the centurion, "Go your way; and as you have believed, so let it be done for you." And his servant was healed that same hour."** Matthew 8:5-13, NKJV.

**Demon-possessed Man Healed:**

They brought a man who was demon-possessed, blind, and mute. Jesus touched him, and the man received healing. The man became set free, and he gained new eyes.

His tongue opened; he started to speak. The great healing of Jesus happened; the people couldn't believe it. They said: Is this man the Son of David?

**"Then one was brought to Him who was demon-possessed, blind and mute; and He healed him, so that the blind and mute man both spoke and saw. And all the multitudes were amazed and said, "Could this be the Son of David?"** Matthew 12:22-23, NKJV.

**Demon-possessed in the Synagogue:**

There was a man with a demon-possessed in the synagogue. Jesus was there; the man saw Him. He shouted, said: leave us alone!

What do we need to do with you, Jesus of Nazareth? Did you come to kill us? You are the Holy One of God.

Jesus began to rebuke him, and He said: **Be quiet!** He commanded an unclean spirit to come out of him.

All demons were shaking the man and tormented him; then, all demons went out of the man. The man set free, and all people were there they said: what is going on?

Is this a new thing! In what authority He commanded the unclean spirit will obey Him and come out of the man? The news spread throughout the regions.

**"But Jesus rebuked him, saying, "Be quiet, and come out of him!" And when the unclean spirit had convulsed him and cried out with a loud voice, he came out of him."** Mark 1:23-28, NKJV.

**An Issue of Blood Woman Healed:**

There was a woman who had an issue of blood in her body for twelve years. She tried all her time, spending her money on physicians and medicine; in fact, her problem grew worse.

But there was no recovery, and she heard that Jesus is coming. She decided to meet Him to get healed. When Jesus was there, she came behind Him.

She said to herself: I may just touch the hem of His garment; I may get healed. Her faith became stronger; the moment she touched Jesus's garment; a direct stream of her blood was withered up.

She felt that something has happened in her body from a long misery illness. Jesus turned around to see who touched His garment.

Jesus's disciples said: they are many people who are around us, we don't know who was touched you?

Jesus knew she was the one who touched His garment. He saw the woman; she fell under His presence; she told Jesus all her sickness stories how she suffered in many years.

Jesus said: your faith has made you whole and go; you are healed from your disease now.

**"For she said, "If only I may touch His clothes, I shall be made well." Immediately the fountain of her blood was dried up, and she felt in her body that she was healed of the affliction."** Mark 5:25-34, NKJV.

**A Paralytic Healed:**

Jesus came to Capernaum, and many people heard that Jesus is in the house. They all gathered in the house, and there was no room for anyone else.

So, some were sitting outside. Jesus taught the Word, and people were hungrily listing the Word of God. Four people carried a paralytic man to his bed, tried to bring him into the house.

But there was so crowded, nor no way to bring him near to Jesus. Finally, these four men took him up to the house, and they uncovered the roof to lay down at the feet of Jesus.

When Jesus saw their faith, how they brought a paralytic man, He said: **Your sins have forgiven you!**

Those Pharisees heard, they said: Only God can forgive sins. Jesus said to them; it is easier to speak to a paralytic man, rise, and you are healed, go home.

A paralytic man stood on his bed and got healed; all people were watching the healing of Jesus. They praised God, and they said: We have not seen such a thing like this?

**"I say to you, arise, take up your bed, and go to your house." Immediately he arose, took up the bed, and went out in the presence of them all, so that all were amazed and glorified God, saying, "We never saw anything like this!"** Mark 2:1-12, NKJV.

### Jesus Cleanses a Leper Man:

When Jesus came to a certain city, there was a man who had full of leprosy on his body. He saw Jesus coming; he fell on his face on the ground.

He asked Jesus; if it's your will, please make me clean. Then Jesus laid His hands on him, and He said: I will.

Immediately, leprosy left the man; he got cleansed and healed completely. Jesus said to him, go, and present yourself to the priest, make an offering to God for cleansing.

**"Then He put out His hand and touched him, saying, "I am willing; be cleansed." Immediately the leprosy left him."** Luke 5:12-14, NKJV.

### Peter's Mother-in-Law Healed:

People were in the synagogue with Jesus. He taught the Word. He left there, and they invited Jesus to Peter's house.

They were asked of Him to look at Peter's mother-in-law, who was sick with a fever. Jesus always had great compassion to heal people.

He went to her and rebuked the fever, and by the voice of Jesus, the fever left her.

She got healed, and she stood up to serve all the guests in the house.

**"So, He stood over her and rebuked the fever, and it left her. And immediately she arose and served them."** Luke 4:38-39, NKJV.

**A Man with Withered Hand Healed:**

On the Sabbath day, Jesus came to the synagogue, and He taught the Word. There was a man who had a right hand withered. The Pharisees, the scribes, and other people were trying to watch Jesus.

What He will do on the Sabbath day. They wanted to find an accusation against Jesus. He said to the man: arise and stand. The man started to stand on his feet.

He said to the scribes and Pharisees: Is it right to save or to destroy life on the Sabbath day.

Then Jesus said to the man: **"Stretch out your hand."** Matthew 12:13, NKJV.

His hand got healed, just like the other one. It made those rulers filled with anger; they went on and discussed what they need to do something about Jesus.

**"And when He had looked around at them all, He said to the man, "Stretch out your hand." And he did so, and his hand was restored as whole as the other."** Luke 6:6-11, NKJV.

**A Demon-possessed Boy Healed:**

There was a large crowd of people who were trying to come near to Jesus. There was a man who had a boy, and he was anxious about his son.

He saw Jesus; he fell on his knees and said to Jesus: Lord, be merciful to my demon-possessed son.

He is falling into the fire and going down into the water, hurting himself, he suffered a lot in his life.

I brought my son to your disciples, but they couldn't heal him. Jesus answered: You, faithless and wicked generation.

How long will I be with you? Jesus had such a love for the boy, and He said: Bring him to me! He just spoke one word: come out of him.

All the demons left him; he became healthy and healed. Then His disciples came to Jesus, asked Him: why we couldn't do this?

Jesus said: because of your unbelief and undoubtedly. If you have faith like a mustard seed, you can move a mountain.

This kind of spirit will need praying and fasting.

**"And Jesus rebuked the demon, and it came out of him; and the child was cured from that very hour."** Matthew 17:14-21, NKJV.

### Bartimaeus Received His Sight:

Jesus came to Jericho with his disciples, and a great multitude followed Him. There was a blind man, Bartimaeus, who heard about Jesus from the crowd.

He had a great desire to get his vision back to see everything around him. *He was able to talk, to able to walk, to be able to move around.*

But the problem he had? He couldn't see. He heard that Jesus of Nazareth came to Jericho; he had such a desire to ask Jesus for healing.

He shouted out for help, but Jesus couldn't hear it, and the people heard his voice, but no one paying attention to him.

He said: Jesus, the Son of David; have mercy on me! The more people urged him to get quiet. His heart stirred up with great excitement to call on Jesus more.

He shouted out loud more: Jesus, have mercy on me. Suddenly, Jesus stopped there.

He listened to the blind man. **"He said: call him here,"** Mark 10:49, NKJV. Jesus's disciples went to him; Jesus calls you: **"Be of great joy, rise." "He is calling you,"** Mark 10:49, NKJV.

He was so excited that Jesus is calling him. He puts aside his garment, and he stood up. He went to Jesus, and He asked the blind man: what do you want me to do for you?

The Bartimaeus said: **"I want to see,"** He said: Go, your faith has healed you. As soon as Jesus told him, he received his sight, and he accompanied Jesus.

**"Then Jesus said to him, "Go your way; your faith has made you well." And immediately he received his sight and followed Jesus on the road."** Mark 10:46-52, NKJV.

**After Sabbath Sunset Many Healed:**

Jesus serves the people until the sun setting down, others brought many sick people. Jesus had such love and care for healing many people.

He could have time to do all things in a short time. He laid His hands on the sick and particular demon-possessed person who has been living for a long time.

Even the demons recognized Jesus, they said: You are the Son of God the Christ. Jesus didn't allow all demons to talk. He rebukes them, cast them all out of people.

And all demons obeyed Jesus to come out of a person's life. People were praising God for healing and miracles.

**"And demons also came out of many, crying out and saying, "You are the Christ, the Son of God!" And He, rebuking them, did not allow them to speak, for they knew that He was the Christ."** Luke 4:40-41, NKJV.

**Many from Seacoast Healed:**

A great multitude of people came throughout the seacoast of Tyre and Sidon, Judah, and Jerusalem. Jesus served people in a large crowd with His disciples, healing all kinds of sickness.

He looked after every person who had an unclean spirit. Jesus knew that they need to get cleaned from a tormented demon spirit.

Jesus rebuked all demons come out of people's life. They were many people trying to touch Jesus to get healed.

When the people near to Jesus, the power of God comes out of Him to heal them.

**"as well as those who were tormented with unclean spirits. And they were healed. And the whole multitude sought to touch Him, for power went out from Him and healed them all."** Luke 6:17-19, NKJV.

**The Compassion of Jesus:**

The more He went into cities and villages throughout the land. Many people heard about the good news of Jesus and followed Him.

His name and His healing miracle became known in many people's hearts. He began to preach and teach the Kingdom of God.

Wherever He went, the healing of Jesus took place. He touched sick people and opened blind eyes and delivered demons-possessed people.

**"Then Jesus went about all the cities and villages, teaching in their synagogues, preaching**

**the gospel of the kingdom, and healing every sickness and every disease among the people."** Matthew 9:35, NKJV.

**People Touched Him, and Made Well:**

Many people traveled from other areas to meet Jesus. They came from everywhere to see Jesus's miracle healing. He was serving and healing people.

They arrived from the land of Gennesaret, and crowded people followed them to the shore. Jesus and others came out of a boat, and people were waiting and looking for Jesus.

People began to see Him and recognized Him. He is the Only One that brings peace and healing.

The Word said: people were bringing their sick, even with bed lay them down at the feet of Jesus. He entered into the marketplaces, cities, villages.

He had a great love and care for all. People wanted to touch His garment to get healed. His presence delivers every evil spirit from the people.

**"Wherever He entered, into villages, cities, or the country, they laid the sick in the**

**marketplaces, and begged Him that they might just touch the hem of His garment. And as many as touched Him were made well."** Mark 6:53-56, NKJV.

**Jesus Healed every Disease:**

After Jesus healed the woman's daughter, he departed from there. He came around the Sea of Galilee; he went up on the mountain; he sat down.

The great multitude was looking for Him; they followed Him again. They brought their sick with the lame, blind, mute, and disabled people.

They laid their loved one down at the feet of Jesus. He touched and healed them all.

Every man could see the blind will receive sight and the lame can walk, and all people worshipped and praised the God of Israel.

**"So, the multitude marveled when they saw the mute speaking, the maimed made whole, the lame walking, and the blind seeing; and they glorified the God of Israel."** Matthew 15:29-31, NKJV.

**Jesus Healed Many at the Temple:**

Jesus enters Jerusalem, people saw Him, they said to themselves, who is He? They said: He is the prophet of the city of Nazareth.

When He approached the temple of God, he saw that people made a temple court a place of marketplaces.

People were selling and buying. He began to overturn the tables of money merchants and the boards of those selling doves.

He said: **"My house shall be called; a house of prayer,"** Matthew 21:13, NKJV.

But you are making it a sanctuary of thieves. The people heard that Jesus came to Jerusalem; they followed Him.

The people showed up with the blind persons and brought the lame to him at the temple, and he healed them all.

**"The blind and the lame came to him at the temple, and he healed them."** Matthew 21:12-14, NKJV.

• CHAPTER 9 •

# The Twelve Disciples Chosen

A TIME FOR CHOOSING the twelve disciples of the Lord Jesus. So, He went up on the mountain; when He came down. He wanted to select the right servant and minister of the Gospel.

Then He chose twelve. He gave them power and to be sent out these men to the mission field. These disciples could deliver those who were demon-possessed.

These are the name of the Lord Jesus's disciples: **"Simon, to whom He gave the name Peter; James the son of Zebedee and John the brother of James, to whom He gave the name Boanerges, that is, "Sons of Thunder"; Andrew, Philip, Bartholomew, Matthew, Thomas, James the son of Alphaeus, Thaddaeus, Simon the**

**Cananite; and Judas Iscariot, who also betrayed Him."** Mark 3:16-19, NKJV.

**Jesus Sending Out the Twelve:**

Jesus called His disciples, those who have been chosen by Him. He assigned them and allowed them to be sent out two by two to preach the Good News.

He gave them the power to cast out every unclean spirit from people's life.

He told them, take nothing for your mission except your staff. He commanded them to take no bags, no bread, no money, and not to wear two shirts. The Lord told them to wear sandals.

He recommended staying where the house will welcome you. You may remain in their home until you leave the town.

If you know any place, you will enter, not listening to you or welcoming you. You may leave that place, shake your dust off your feet, and the day of judgment will come on them.

So, these disciples went out and preached the Word of Salvation. People heard the Salvation of the Lord, and they repented their sins.

They had the power of God to cast out demons; they anointed sick people with oil.

They healed those who were suffering from sickness in the name of the Lord Jesus.

**"So, they went out and preached that people should repent. And they cast out many demons, and anointed with oil many who were sick, and healed them."** Mark 6:7-13, NKJV.

**Disciples Couldn't Cast Out the Unclean Spirit:**

Jesus was in the middle of a crowd; the people were happy to see Him. A father had a son who was a mute spirit.

Whenever the spirit seizes him, it drives him down; he foams at his mouth, grinds his teeth together, and grows into harsh.

So, the father said, I talked to Your disciples, but they couldn't cast it out. Jesus said: **unbelief generation, how long will I be with you?**

He told the father to bring his son. The moment the boy came near to Jesus, the evil spirit was living inside the boy could recognize Jesus.

The spirit tormented him; he went down and rolling on the ground and foaming at his mouth.

Jesus asked the boy's father; how long your son has been living in this condition, the father answered: since from his childhood!

The father said: sometimes the spirit will throw him into the fire and into the water to kill him, please be merciful to him and help him.

Jesus said: if you believe anything can happen. The father's boy realized that he had an unbelieving heart, and tears came out of his eyes and said: Lord, **help my unbelief.**

Jesus saw many people were watching, and they will see the power of God. He told the unclean spirit to come out of him, will not enter his life again.

The unclean spirit cried out, and the boy laid down as dead. The people saw the boy, they said: **the boy is dead.**

Then Jesus took his hands, helped him to stand on his feet. He gave the boy to his father.

Later on, all His disciples asked Him: why couldn't we cast out the unclean spirit. He answered, remember, this kind of spirit will need praying and fasting.

**"And when He had come into the house, His disciples asked Him privately, "Why could we not cast it out?" So, He said to them, "This kind can come out by nothing but prayer and fasting."** Mark 9:17-29, NKJV.

**Jesus Forbid no One:**

One of the disciples, John came to Jesus asked: Teacher, we saw someone casting out demons in your name. We forbade him, and because he is not following us.

Jesus answered: Do not forbid him, for anyone who performs a miracle in My name will be able quickly afterward to talk evil of me.

The one who stands with us is not against us is on our side. He said: For whoever offers you a drink of water in My name because you believe in Christ.

I declare to you, and he will not lose his reward. Mark 9:38-41.

**"Do not forbid him, for no one who works a miracle in My name can soon afterward speak evil of Me."** Mark 9:38-41, NKJV.

**Jesus Sent His Disciples to Preach:**

Jesus promised to His disciples that they preach the Good News, and these signs and wonders will accompany those who believe.

Jesus handed over the power to them, to cast out demons in His name, speak with new tongues, pick up snakes.

If you see someone who drinks any poison, it will not hurt or harm him.

They will lay hands on sick people will receive healing in their body in Jesus's name.

**"these signs will follow those who believe: In My name they will cast out demons; they will speak with new tongues."** Mark 16:17-18, NKJV.

**Jesus Sent out 70 (or 72):**

The Lord chose seventy and others. The Lord instructed his disciples on their journey of a mission field. Where He was about to leave, he allowed them to go out two by two to every city.

He said: The harvest is plentiful, but the workers are few. When you go your way, carry nothing with you, when you go to any city. Where a house receives you, you may stay there, eat and drink over.

First, you would say: peace in this house, if the house gets your peace, it is not, your peace will return to you.

If a home welcomes you to stay, to eat, and drink because the worker is worthy of his wages. If you see any sick, lay your hands on them, speak healing in my name that shall get healed.

Proclaim **"the Kingdom of God is at hand,"** Mark 1:15, NKJV.

These seventy followers came back from the mission task that the Lord Jesus gave them.

They brought an excellent report: Lord, we speak your name, even demons know you and obeying in your name.

Jesus said: I saw Satan was falling like lightning from heaven. He said to them, I gave you authority to preach the Word.

You will overcome over any demonic spirit, and over any enemy, nothing will hurt you.

But remember not rejoicing for this, be glad that your name is written in the book of life in heaven.

**"Nevertheless, do not rejoice in this, that the spirits are subject to you, but rather rejoice because your names are written in heaven."** Luke 10:17-20, NKJV.

**False Prophets With "Signs and Wonders":**

The Lord Jesus warned His disciples to be aware of such false prophets and false Christs. He instructed them about, if anyone says, oh, Christ is coming and performing miracles.

Jesus said: There will have false prophets and teachers. False Christ will rise in the future would deceive you and show their signs and wonders to persuade you to believe, but do not believe them.

**"For false Christs and false prophets shall rise, and shall shew signs and wonders, to seduce, if it were possible, even the elect."** Mark 13:21-22, NKJV.

**Jesus' Grieves over Jerusalem:**

The Herod's plan to kill Jesus, so, some Pharisees came to Jesus to warn Him. They told Him: get out of here. Herod will be trying to find you and kill you.

Jesus said, go and tell Herod; I will heal the sick and cast out demons out today and tomorrow. I will finish my course on the third day.

**"Go, tell that fox, Behold, I cast out demons and perform cures today and tomorrow, and the third day I shall be perfected."** Luke 13:31-32, NKJV.

• CHAPTER 10 •

# Healing & Miracles of the Apostles

When Jesus ascended to heaven, He anointed His disciples with the power of the Holy Spirit to preach and teach the Word.

The disciples of Jesus became very faithful to remain loyal in their faith and having confidence in His Word. They have chosen by the direction of the Holy Spirit.

The Lord Jesus developed into their spiritual potentials, talents, gifts, and made them great Apostles.

They became the Apostles of Jesus to preach the Good News to establish the church for the Lord Jesus. They received the power to do phenomena; so that their congregations would accept their teaching.

They preached by the power of God who can hear the Word and would believe that Jesus is the Son of God. Receive Jesus as the Savior of sinners.

God has operated miracles and healing through all His servants to manifest His Glory to the people.

These Apostles knew it would be not finished their task for preaching after more servants will come to preach the Good news to the whole world.

Miracles and healing were a platform for the Apostles to reach out to lost souls bring them into the Kingdom of God.

The miracles and healing of Jesus are available here today for all of us. Jesus said, you just believe nothing impossible with God.

The Apostle Paul was an intelligent Jew, a Pharisee, and a devoted person of his belief. He preached the Gospel to the Gentile people of the Roman world.

He became a faithful Christian and serving in the early Christian church. We would gratify that someone like Paul of Tarsus grow into a witness for Christ.

**A Paralyzed Man from Birth Healed:**

There was a man born lame since his birth. They carried him to sit down to the temple gate called: Beautiful. He sat down every day, and he was asking people for money to survive day after day.

When Peter and John tried to enter the temple, he looked at them and asked for money. Peter and John stopped there in front of him.

They looked at his eyes, and Peter said: look at us, I don't have gold and silver to give it to you.

But stand your feet and walk in the name of Jesus of Nazareth. Peter took his hand with his right hand; his feet and ankles were getting stronger and stood on his feet.

He jumped up with joy and walked. He started to worship and praise God. People have seen him around the area.

They said: this man was lame; he is sitting at the temple gate called: Beautiful. He got healed, and there was an amazing miracle that happened in front of their eyes.

**"Then Peter said, "Silver and gold I do not have, but what I do have I give you: In the name of Jesus Christ of Nazareth, rise up and walk."** Acts 3:2-10, NKJV.

**Peter and John Prayed for Boldness:**

Peter and John were standing to preach the resurrection of Jesus, and they preached the Word with the power of God.

There is no other name that has been given to us except the name of Jesus we shall be saved. The elders and priests of the temple were anxious, and they tried to stop Peter and John.

They took them to jail until the next day when the elders and the ruler of the law came to the temple, they brought Peter and John.

They asked: **In what power and what name do you do this?** Then Peter said by the anointing of the Holy Spirit: **By the name of Jesus Christ of Nazareth,** that you crucified Him, and He raised again.

So, these elders found nothing to accuse them, and they ordered to let them go free.

But others came saying; if these men go back to the people in Jerusalem, they have made signs and wonders, they will do again.

The elders threatened them, said to Peter and John, you may go, but you will promise not to use the name of Jesus again.

They said: we cannot help it because of what we have seen and what we heard of the name of Jesus! Peter and John back to their members in the congregation.

They prayed with boldness. They prayed, Lord, send your mighty Spirit to heal the sick and save your lost souls.

After this prayer: they went to preach the Eternal Word of God with signs and wonders. They preached with a great boldness never before.

May your anointing of the Holy Spirit shall come down to us to preach the salvation of the Lord.

**"After they prayed, the place where they were meeting was shaken. And they were all filled with the Holy Spirit and spoke the word of God boldly."** Acts 4:31, NKJV.

**Peter's Shadow Healed the Sick:**

Throughout the cities, Peter was preaching the Good News of Jesus, when Peter passed by in Solomon's Porch. People heard and knew that Peter is coming and passing by this way.

The people brought their sick men and women, demon-possessed, lame on their bed, and with all kinds of infirmities laid down on the street.

When Peter was walking and passing by, they were hoping his shadow was falling over these sick people, and they will get healed.

People coming from all around Jerusalem and other cities heard about signs and wonders of the Lord through Peter.

**"so that they brought the sick out into the streets and laid them on beds and couches, that at least the shadow of Peter passing by might fall on some of them."** Acts 5:15, NKJV.

**Apostles released from Prison by an Angel:**

The high priest, along with a group of the sect of the Sadducees, stood against the Apostles. They became very furious with them.

They ordered their arrest and put them into prison. At midnight the angel of the Lord appeared to the Apostles in prison.

The angel said to them; Go to preach in the temple about the life of Jesus. **"Go, stand in the**

**temple, and speak to the people all the words of this life."**

They got freed, next day, they went into the temple began to speak the Word and teach about the Kingdom of God.

At the same time, the high priest came back to call prisoners. They went to bring prisoners to the leaders, and they could find no one in prison.

They came back to give the high priest the report that those prisoners are not there. They said: We had security at the prison door.

We don't know how they got out of there. Others came to the high priest, saying; we saw those Apostles were in prison.

Now they are standing in the temple preaching and teaching the Word of God.

**"Look, the men whom you put in prison are standing in the temple and teaching the people!"** Acts 5:17-25, NKJV.

**Lying to the Holy Spirit:**

There was a couple named Ananias, with his wife, Sapphira. They had a property and then sold a piece of land to offer to the congregation for the work of God.

They both agreed to keep a portion of the money, and the rest of the money to give to leaders of the church.

However, Peter had acknowledged it by his spirit, and the Lord revealed to him that Ananias is not speaking the truth.

So, Ananias came, he brought the money and laid it down as an offering. Peter said: **Why did you Ananias lie in your heart to the Holy Spirit.**

You kept a portion of the money for yourself. And you brought half of the money and offering to the Lord. You tried to lie to man, but you cannot lie to God.

Ananias heard these things from Peter. He fell down and gave his last breath and died. They came to take him away and buried him.

After three hours later, his wife Sapphira arrived; she didn't know what happened to Ananias.

Peter asked her, that's all money that you have sold from a piece of land and offering to the Lord. Sapphira agreed; yes, that's money we sold it and offering all to the Lord.

Peter said: How can be you both agreed to lie to the Lord. At the same time, they carried your husband and buried him, and they have also carried you out at the door.

She heard it and fell down in front of them and died. They carried her out to bury her as well.

**"Ananias, why has Satan filled your heart to lie to the Holy Spirit and keep back part of the price of the land for yourself?"** Acts 5:1-10, NKJV.

**Stephen Martyred for Jesus:**

As we recognize a man of faith and power. Stephen, who had such desired to walk in signs and wonders among people in those days.

Some people rose against Stephen called, Synagogue of the Freedmen.

These Jews groups from Cyrene and Alexandria and also from the provinces of Cilicia and Asia gathered together to argue with Stephen.

These groups were hearing the word of wisdom that Stephen has spoken to them.

So, they began to say against his speech. They secretly induced some and stirred them up to come against Stephen.

They said: we have heard Stephen spoken blasphemous words about Moses and God. The elders and leaders began to attack Stephen and take him to the council meeting.

They tried to make some false statements against Stephen. By saying, he spoke blasphemous words against our Holy place and our law.

They were saying: He spoke that Jesus of Nazareth came to destroy the temple to change and to make the custom of Moses.

All council members in the meeting looking at Stephen's face, realized his face like the face of an angel.

The power of God came upon Stephen. He preached in the meeting. He spoke about there was a call of God for Abraham; he became the father of faith.

He mentioned after 400 years of slavery in Egypt. God heard the cry of His people Israel. He sent Moses to deliver from the bondage of Pharaoh.

And the people of God Israel rebelled against God again. He focused on the people of Israel that you resisted the Holy Spirit.

After everyone heard the testimony of Stephen, they became raged and furious.

Saul, whose name is Paul, ordered the killing of Stephen, and he was there at the time of his martyrdom.

But Stephen was filled with the anointing of the Holy Spirit, **"he saw the Glory of God in heaven,"** Acts 7:55, NKJV.

He saw Jesus sitting at the right hand of the Father. The people taking out of the meeting in the city and stoned him.

He opened up his eyes and said: Lord, receive my spirit. He fell down on his knees, cried out. Lord, do not charge them for their sins. *He fell asleep.*

**"Then he knelt down and cried out with a loud voice, "Lord, do not charge them with this sin." And when he had said this,** he fell asleep." Acts 7:30, NKJV.

**Philip Preached in Samaria:**

Saul began to persecute the church, all believers in the Lord were scarred around the land. Philip went to Samaria to preach the Good News.

The Lord Jesus moved powerfully in that city with signs and wonders followed Philip.

He cast out unclean spirits; he was rebuking with a loud voice to demons that came out of many people who were possessed.

Many who were crippled, disabled, and the power of God healed the lame. And the people have seen the healing and miracles of Jesus, and great joy came in that city.

**"For unclean spirits, crying with a loud voice, came out of many who were possessed; and many who were paralyzed, and lame were healed."** Acts 8:4-8, NKJV.

**An Ethiopian Baptized by Philip:**

An angel of the Lord spoke to Philip to go down south toward Jerusalem and Gaza in the desert. There was a man a eunuch of higher authority is coming from Ethiopia.

He was under Candace the queen of the Ethiopians; he was an important man in charge of her treasury. An angel gave these details to Philip about an Ethiopian.

So, An Ethiopian traveled to Jerusalem to worship. He was sitting in his chariot, and he had a desire to read about the book of Isaiah.

The spirit said to Philip, go to him; he went there and sitting in his chariot. Philip asked him; **Do you understand?**

What are you reading? An Ethiopian answered, how can I know unless someone can explain to me?

Philip sits down next to him, and he was meditating on the book of Isaiah. An Ethiopian asked him: this verse is to whom talking about himself or someone else.

So, Philip preached to him about Jesus, and they came near to water. Philip asked him, do you want to get baptized in the water now.

An Ethiopian said, yes, I will, and I get baptized here. Philip asked him: **"do you believe Jesus is the Messiah?"**

He answered, Yes, I believe. He told the chariot to stop, they both got out and went down into the water, Philip baptized him.

The moment an Ethiopian came out of the water, the Spirit took Philip away. He didn't see him anymore; an Ethiopian began rejoicing in the salvation of the Lord.

However, after Philip ministered to an Ethiopian, he showed up at Azotus. He traveled to preach the gospel in all the cities until he came to Caesarea.

**"He was led as a sheep to the slaughter; And as a lamb before its shearer is silent, So He opened not His mouth."** Acts 8:32, NKJV.

**"And both Philip and the eunuch went down into the water, and he baptized him"**. Acts 8:26-40, NKJV.

### Healing by Philip in Samaria:

Saul persecuted many Christian believers. Therefore, they have scattered around, preaching the Word of God.

Philip traveled down to the city of Samaria; he preached and taught the Word there. The people were hungry and thirsty, hearing about the Kingdom of God.

The Lord Jesus made miracles, and those who were crippled, and lame healed through Philip.

He cast out an unclean spirit with a loud voice to come out of many people. The multitudes of people who were demons-possessed were free from all evil spirits.

**"And the multitudes with one accord heeded the things spoken by Philip, hearing and seeing the miracles which he did,"** Acts 8:4-7, NKJV.

**Aeneas Healed by Peter:**

As Peter traveled throughout the land, he came down to the congregation. He met some believers who were staying in Lydda.

There was a man Aeneas, who became paralyzed; he had an infirmity for eight years.

Peter stood in front of him, tell him, Aeneas; Jesus heals you now. You may rise and stand up and take your bed. He stood up and got cured.

All the people were in Lydda saw the healing of Jesus, how Aeneas received his healing; they all came to know the Lord.

**"Peter said to him, Aeneas, Jesus the Christ heals you. Arise and make your bed. Then he arose immediately."** Acts 9:32-35, NKJV.

**Tabitha Turned to Life:**

As there was a woman who was a disciple named Tabitha, she had the heart to do charitable deeds. She has done excellent work for the Lord at Joppa.

What happened; after a while, she got sick and died. Other people washed her body, take her to the upper room.

Meanwhile, Peter was in Lydda; some knew that Peter could still be there. They sent a message with two men to Peter to tell him about Tabitha.

They found Peter, and he came quickly with these two men to Joppa. They took Peter to the upper room, where Tabitha laid down dead.

All the widows and other women were grieving over Tabitha. When Peter arrived in the upper room, he took all the women out of the room.

Then he kneeled and prayed. He looked at Tabitha's body said: Tabitha arise. Suddenly she opened her eyes, she saw who is there, and saw Peter.

She sat down. Peter took her hands and lifted her up. She stood on her feet. Peter called all women to come in and to see Tabitha is alive.

The healing and miracles happened throughout all Joppa. Because of the miracles from the dead to life happened, many believed in the Lord Jesus.

**"But Peter put them all out and knelt down and prayed. And turning to the body he said, Tabitha, arise. And she opened her eyes, and when she saw Peter she sat up."** Acts 9:36-42, NKJV.

### Saul's Conversion in Damascus:

Saul was a religious man; he wanted to find a way to wipe out all Christian believers and disciples of Jesus. He threatened many believers in every city in the land to arrest them.

He went to the high priest; requested a letter for going to the synagogues of Damascus.

He will find more Christian believers and disciples over there to bring back to Jerusalem to get them killed.

So, he began his journey along with other men, while he was on the road-going near Damascus, there was a light shone around him, and he fell on the ground.

A voice came, and he heard saying: **"Saul, Saul, why are you persecuting Me?"** Acts 9:4, NKJV. He was shaking and greatly surprised to hear the voice of the Lord Jesus.

Saul asked the Lord, what do you want me to do? The Lord said: get up and go to the city, you will be told what to do!

These men were with Saul, they heard the voice. But they didn't see anyone around them; they were astonished.

Saul stood up; these men helped him and taking him to Damascus. Because he couldn't see well, he didn't eat and drink for three days.

There was a disciple of Jesus in the city of Damascus named Ananias. The Lord spoke to him in the vision to go to Saul: You must go to find the house of Judah, the street called Straight in the city.

You will ask a man from Tarsus named Saul, and he is praying. Ananias asked the Lord in the vision: Lord, he is the one who was persecuting many Christians in Jerusalem and killed them.

He was trying to arrest more believers from the church. The Lord answered him: He is my chosen one; he will serve and preach the Gospel to Gentiles in my name.

I will reveal to him how many things he must go through with crises in my name.

Ananias went and obeyed the Lord, he found the house, he met Saul. He prayed for Saul and laid hands on him. He said to Saul: The Lord Jesus appeared to you on the road to Damascus.

Now he sent me to you that I may lay my hands on you that you may receive your healing. You may be filled with the Holy Spirit.

Immediately, something like scales fell off of his eyes.

He received his sight back; he got up and baptized there. Some believers served Saul with food; he got his strength back; he spent a few days with believers there in Damascus.

**"Go, for he is a chosen vessel of Mine to bear My name before Gentiles, kings, and the children of Israel."** Acts 9:1-19, NKJV.

**An Angel Delivered Peter from Prison:**

King Herod began to find more Christian believers to kill them. In fact, he killed James, the brother of John. Herod wanted to please the Jews to hurt Christian believers.

He found Peter and tried to kill him as well. But it was the Feast of Unleavened Bread. So, he couldn't do it, and then King Herod put Peter in prison.

He ordered a tied four corner secured around him in prison that he will not escape.

On the other side, the church members were praying for Peter. The night before King Herod, he wanted to bring back for the next day to stand in front of people for his charges.

Peter was sleeping, bound with chains with two other soldiers and the guards beside him. An angel of the Lord came up, and a light shone into prison and standing in front of Peter.

The angel woke Peter up by his side; he said to him: Get up quickly, all his chains fall off of his hands. He put on his clothes and sandals.

The angel said to Peter: put on your garment and follow me! Peter didn't even know what is going on with him, where the angel is trying to lead him where to go?

Peter thought he saw a vision. He didn't know; it was a real angel, and the angel is trying to help him escape from prison.

The angel and Peter were together; they passed the first guard post, and they passed the second guard posts. Then they came to the third guard called the iron gate to open up to enter the city.

The angel led him into the safe street; he departed from him, and Peter was by himself alone.

Peter just came to himself, and he did not see any vision. It was a real experience with an angel; he helped him to get out of prison. He said: Truly the Lord sent an angel to deliver me.

**"an angel of the Lord stood by him, and a light shone in the prison; and he struck Peter on the side and raised him up, saying, "Arise quickly!" And his chains fell off his hands."** Acts 12:1-11, NKJV.

**Peter Freed entered the House of Prayer:**

An angel made a way to help Peter escape the prison. Peter was walking in the night found himself alone when an angel of the Lord left him.

He knew that he must go to the house of Mary. The mother of John Mark they were praying for Peter with other members of the Congregation.

No one expected it, the Lord answered the prayer quickly. Peter stood at the door and knocking.

The girl's name Rhoda came to the door, she heard the voice of Peter, but she was so excited, she didn't open the door.

The girl went back into the house said, there is a voice I hear outside the sound like Peter. Then Peter was still knocking at the door.

Finally, they came to open the door for Peter. They were all happy to see him. Peter shared how the Lord sent an angel to deliver him from prison.

He said: go and tell brethren, and James also to leave the place. When the daytime arrived, and King Herod heard that Peter is not there, and he escaped from Prison.

He was furious and ordered all guards, and soldiers were guarding on the night in prison with Peter should be killed. King Heron searched for Peter but couldn't find him.

**"where many were gathered together praying."** Acts 12:12-19, NKJV.

### Paul and Barnabas Sent out to Mission:

There was a congregation with prophets, and teachers were serving the people in Antioch. They were such a powerful presence of God, and people could see the manifestation of the Holy Spirit.

They had worship service and began to praise the Lord. The Holy Spirit said: Barnabas and Paul have called into the mission work; they send them out.

After praying and fasting, the leaders laid hands on Barnabas and Paul and send them to preach the Good News. They traveled to Seleucia and sailed from there to Cyprus.

When they got there in Salamis, they went there. They met a Jewish sorcerer who was using power gained from evil spirits and a false prophet named Bar-Jesus.

He was a person with the proconsul, Sergius Paulus. The proconsul sent a message to Barnabas and Paul to come to his place to speak about the Word of God.

The Jewish sorcerer names Elymas was opposed to their visit. He didn't want the proconsul to hear the Word, and not having faith in God.

Then Paul was filled with the Holy Spirit, and he looked straight at him. Paul said: you are a child of the devil, and you are full of lies and deception. You cannot hold back the work of the Lord Jesus.

Paul said: the hand of the Lord is coming against you. You will be blind now, and you cannot see the light of the sun.

Immediately he became blind, and he couldn't see anything, he was looking for someone to lead him.

**"And now, indeed, the hand of the Lord is upon you, and you shall be blind, not seeing the sun for a time,"** Acts 13:1-11, NKJV.

### Cripple Man Healed by Paul:

Paul and the other apostles came to the Lycaonian cities of Lystra and Derbe. They arrived there in Lystra to minister in the town.

Paul began to preach the Word, and the power of God was poured out on Paul and gathering of people who were listing to the Word of God.

There was a man who was a born cripple from his mother's womb, and he never walked in his life. He was listing to the preaching of Paul.

He had a great desire to walk, but Paul built good faith in his heart. Paul saw him and observing him very carefully.

Paul sees in his spirit that the cripple man has faith to get healed now.

So, Paul came to him and said in a loud voice: **"Stand up straight on your feet!"** He stood up, and he got healed, he walked and praising God. Acts 14:8-10, NKJV.

### An Earthquake shook, Paul and Silas Freed:

When Paul and Silas were going to the house of Prayer in the city. There was a slave girl who had a spirit of divination. She saw them and followed them wherever Paul and Silas were going!

She said: these men of God will proclaim the salvation of God to us. She did several days follow them in the marketplaces.

Finally, Paul got annoyed by her coming back and disturbing their ministry. Paul commended the spirit come out of her in the name of Jesus Christ.

When the girls' master was trying to send out a slave girl to do business in the street. He got angry and attacked Paul and Silas dragged them into the house of authorities.

They found the magistrates, and they said: these men are Jews, brought problems to our city. He said, they are trying to teach a new law that is not lawful for us.

So many people heard about them, they all stood up against Paul and Silas. The magistrates got furious and commanded to beat them with rods and put them in prison.

They took them into prison, tied their feet with chains. At night Paul and Silas were worshipping, praising God with songs, and singing hymns in prison.

All other prisoners around are listing to them. Suddenly there was an earthquake shook the foundation of the prison. Then all prison doors unlocked, and Paul and Silas's chains around their feet loosed.

The guard woke up from sleeping; he saw the door opened, and he thought all prisoners escaped. He took his sword to attack; he wanted to kill himself.

Paul said to him: we are doing fine; don't hurt yourself. He got a light; he ran into prison and fell at the feet of Paul, what do I need to get saved?

Paul said: believe the Lord Jesus, you and your household shall be saved? He believed along with all his family, and they rejoice in the salvation of the Lord Jesus.

The magistrates found out to let these men go! The prisoner guard went to Paul said: the magistrates wanted to let you go, and you are free to go.

Paul said we would not go anywhere. They have beaten us in public as a Roman citizen condemned us unjustly, and they put us in prison.

Paul said: Let the magistrates come by themselves, let us out of here. So, the magistrates heard they are Romans. Then they showed up and asked them.

You are free to go, led them out. Paul and Silas went to Lydia, and they were glad to see them; they encouraged them; they went to another city.

**"Suddenly there was a great earthquake, so that the foundations of the prison were shaken; and immediately all the doors were opened, and everyone's chains were loosed."** Acts 16:16-40, NKJV.

**Paul's Handkerchiefs Healed the Sick:**

The Lord has effectively used Paul in the synagogue for three months, preaching the Word boldly.

Some heard were believing in the heart; some didn't believe and spoke the evil against the Way front of the people.

He left those who were against the Way; he taught the Word in the school of Tyrannus. His preaching and teaching went on for two years.

Others are also serving and preaching the Word to all Asia regions. Paul ministered to all people from the Jews and Greeks who will hear the Word of the Lord.

Now God has made an enormous miracle and healing by the hands of Paul. Even handkerchiefs from Paul's body brought to the sick people they received their healing.

When handkerchiefs or aprons touched the sick, all demons left, all diseases of people were gone, healed in the name of Jesus.

**"Now God worked unusual miracles by the hands of Paul, so that even handkerchiefs or aprons were brought from his body to the sick, and the diseases left them, and the evil spirits went out of them."** Acts 19:11-12, NKJV.

### Paul Healed A man Fell through Window:

Paul traveled many different directions for preaching until he stopped in Troas. On his first day of the visit, when all disciples got together. They were broken bread and enjoyed in God's presence.

Paul began to speak and teach the Word of God, and he went on for the whole day until midnight.

They had some light in the upper room, and everyone was trying to be awakening, not fall into sleep. There were all sitting and listing to Paul.

Especially a young man named Eutychus, and he was sitting next to the window; he got tired, fell asleep. Then he fell off of the window down from the third floor on the ground.

They went to see what happened to him; they found him dead. Paul reached down to him. He saw him, and he is dead; he said: don't worry, his life in His hands.

Paul fell on him and put his arms around Eutychus. He became alive again, and members of the congregation were blessed that he came back to life again.

Paul went up to eat and continued to preach and teach the Word until the next day. Then he departed from there.

**"But Paul went down, fell on him, and embracing him said, "Do not trouble yourselves, for his life is in him."** Acts 20:7-12, NKJV.

**Paul Bits by Snack in Malta:**

After the storm on the sea, finally, all crews needed to survive by the strong wind and the rain, which the ship got damaged.

Paul, along with all soldiers and prisoners on the ship. Then laid themselves on every piece of the ship, swimming toward the shore.

They arrived at the land Malta. They met the native people from the island; they found the people are very kind and friendly.

They welcome them, so, the day they arrived in Malta. It was raining poured out, and it became freezing. They made a fire to get warm, they all gathered around the fire.

Paul had a bundle of sticks to put on fire. Suddenly, a snake came out of the fire, bits at the hand of Paul.

The people saw him; they were watching him. They said: this is a killer; he came out of the sea. He needed justice; the goddess will not allow him to live.

They looked at him, his hand going to swell up and going to die. But Paul shook his hand off the snake, throw it out into the fire again.

All the people watching Paul and, but nothing happened. They changed their mind; they said: he is a god.

**"But Paul shook the snake off into the fire and suffered no ill effects."** Acts 28:1-6, NKJV.

### Publius's Father Healed by Paul:

Paul stayed on the island before sailing to Rome. There was an estate owned by the chief official of the island named Publius. He invited Paul to stay, who made them welcome and treated them with entertainment for three days.

On this occasion, the father of Publius was very sick of a fever and dysentery. Paul went to him; he prayed and laid hands on him. He received his healing by the power of God.

All people heard about the healing of Publius's father; the people of the island brought their loved ones who received healing as well.

Paul ministered to them; he prayed and laid his hands on them. God touched and restored them all.

They were all overjoyed in the miracles of God. Paul stayed for several days again.

The people and Publius were very generously provided their needs for them in their journey. They sailed by ship along with others to Rome.

**"And it happened that the father of Publius lay sick of a fever and dysentery. Paul went in to him and prayed, and he laid his hands on him and healed him"** Acts 28:7-10, NKJV.

• CHAPTER 11 •

# Healing Scriptures in the Old Testament

- "I will put none of the diseases on you which I have brought on the Egyptians. **For I am the Lord who heals you.**" Exodus 15:26, NKJV.
- "So, you shall serve the Lord your God, and He will bless your bread and your water. And **I will take sickness away from the midst of you**" Exodus 23:25, NKJV.
- "So, Moses cried out to the Lord, saying, **"Please heal her, O God, I pray!"** Numbers 12:13, NKJV.
- "**the Lord will take away from you all sickness,**" Deuteronomy 7:15, NKJV.

- "Return and tell Hezekiah the leader of My people, 'Thus says the Lord, the God of David your father: **I have heard your prayer, I have seen your tears; surely I will heal you.**" 2 Kings 20:5, NKJV.
- "if My people who are called by My name will humble themselves, and pray and seek My face, and turn from their wicked ways, then I will hear from heaven, and will forgive their sin and **heal their land**." 2 Chronicles 7:14, NKJV.
- "Have mercy on me, O Lord, for I am weak; **O Lord, heal me**, for my bones are troubled." Psalm 6:2, NKJV.
- "O Lord my God, I cried out to You, And **You healed me.**" Psalm 30:2, NKJV.
- "He guards all his bones; **Not one of them is broken**." Psalm 34:20, NKJV.
- "The Lord will strengthen him on his bed of illness; You will sustain him **on his sickbed**. I said, "Lord, be merciful to me; **Heal my soul**, for I have sinned against You." Psalm 41:3-4, NKJV.
- "I said, "Lord, be merciful to me; **Heal my soul**, for I have sinned against You." Psalm 41:4, NKJV.

- "Who forgives all your iniquities, **Who heals all your diseases**," Psalm 103:3, NKJV.
- "**He sent His word and healed them**, And delivered them from their destructions." Psalms 107:20, NKJV.
- "**I shall not die, but live**, And declare the works of the Lord." Psalm 118:17, NKJV.
- "**He heals the brokenhearted**, and binds up their wounds." Psalm 147:3, NKJV.
- "Pleasant words are like a honeycomb, **Sweetness to the soul and health** to the bones." Proverbs 16:24, NKJV.
- "**A merry heart does good, like medicine**, but a broken spirit dries the bones." Proverbs 17:22, NKJV.
- "A time to kill, And **a time to heal**; A time to break down, And a time to build up." Ecclesiastes 3:3, NKJV.
- "And the Lord will strike Egypt, He will strike and heal it; they will return to the Lord, and He will be entreated by them and **heal them**." Isaiah 19:22, NKJV.
- "But He was wounded for our transgressions, He was bruised for our iniquities; The chastisement for our peace was upon

Him, And **by His stripes we are healed.**" Isaiah 53:5, NKJV.

- "O Lord, by these things men live; And in all these things is the life of my spirit; So, **You will restore me and make me live.**" Isaiah 38:16, NKJV.
- "I have seen his ways, and **will heal him**; I will also lead him, And restore comforts to him, And to his mourners. "I create the fruit of the lips: Peace, peace to him who is far off and to him who is near," Says the Lord, "And **I will heal him**." Isaiah 57:18-19, NKJV.
- "Then your light shall break forth like the morning, **Your healing shall spring forth speedily,** And your righteousness shall go before you; The glory of the Lord shall be your rear guard." Isaiah 58:8, NKJV.
- "Heal me, O Lord, and **I shall be healed**; Save me, and I shall be saved, For You are my praise." Jeremiah 17:14, NKJV.
- "For **I will restore health to you, And heal you of your wounds**,' says the Lord." Jeremiah 30:17, NKJV.
- "Behold, **I will bring it health and healing; I will heal them** and reveal to them the

abundance of peace and truth." Jeremiah 33:6, NKJV.

- CHAPTER 12 -

# Healing Scriptures in the New Testament

- "Jesus went about all Galilee, teaching in their synagogues, preaching the gospel of the kingdom, and **healing all kinds of sickness** and **all kinds of disease** among the people." Matthew 4:23, NKJV.
- "But Jesus turned around, and when He saw her He said, "Be of good cheer, daughter; **your faith has made you well**." And the woman was made well from that hour." Matthew 9:22, NKJV.
- "when He had called His twelve disciples to Him, He gave them power over unclean spirits, to cast them out, and **to heal**

**all kinds of sickness** and **all kinds of disease.**" Matthew 10:1, NKJV.
- "**Heal the sick,** cleanse the lepers, raise the dead, cast out demons. Freely you have received, freely give." Matthew 10:8, NKJV.
- "And great multitudes followed Him, and **He healed them there**." Matthew 19:2, NKJV.
- "When Jesus heard it, He said to them, "Those who are well have no need of a physician, **but those who are sick**. I did not come to call the righteous, but sinners, to repentance." Mark 2:17, NKJV.
- "and begged Him earnestly, saying, "My little daughter lies at the point of death. Come and lay Your hands on her, that **she may be healed**, and she will live." Mark 5:23, NKJV.
- "And He said to her, "Daughter, **your faith** has made you well. Go in peace, and **be healed of your affliction**." Mark 5:34, NKJV.
- "And they cast out many demons, and **anointed with oil many who were sick, and healed them.**" Mark 6:13, NKJV.

- "Jesus said to him, "If you can believe, **all things are possible to him who believes.**" Mark 9:23, NKJV.
- "Now it happened on a certain day, as He was teaching, that there were Pharisees and teachers of the law sitting by, who had come out of every town of Galilee, Judea, and Jerusalem. And **the power of the Lord was present to heal them**." Luke 5:17, NKJV.
- "And the whole multitude sought to touch Him, **for power went out from Him and healed them all.**" Luke 6:19, NKJV.
- "But Jesus said, "**Somebody touched Me**, for I perceived power going out from Me." Luke 8:46, NKJV.
- "And **heal the sick there**, and say to them, 'The kingdom of God has come near to you.'" Luke 10:9, NKJV.
- "He laid His hands on her, and **immediately she was made straight**, and glorified God." Luke 13:13, NKJV.
- "But they kept silent. And **He took him and healed him**, and let him go." Luke 14:4, NKJV.

- "And He said to him, Arise, go your way. **Your faith has made you well.**" Luke 17:19, NKJV.
- Jesus said to him, "**Rise, take up your bed and walk.**" John 5:8, NKJV.
- "they should understand with their hearts and turn, So, that **I should heal them**" John 12:40, NKJV.
- "**by stretching out Your hand to heal**, and that signs and wonders may be done through the name of Your holy Servant Jesus." Acts 4:30, NKJV.
- "And Peter said to him, "Aeneas, **Jesus the Christ heals you**. Arise and make your bed." Then he arose immediately." Acts 9:34, NKJV.
- "how in the town Spirit and with power, who went about doing good and **healing all who were oppressed by the devil**, for God was with Him." Acts 10:38, NKJV.
- "Is anyone among you sick? Let him call for the elders of the church, and let them pray over him, anointing him with oil in the name of the Lord. And **the prayer of faith will save the sick**, and the Lord will raise him up. And if he has committed

sins, he will be forgiven." James 5:14-15, NKJV.
- "Confess your trespasses to one another, and pray for one another, **that you may be healed.** The effective, fervent prayer of a righteous man avails much." James 5:16, NKJV.
- "who Himself bore our sins in His own body on the tree, that we, having died to sins, might live for righteousness—**by whose stripes you were healed**" 1 Peter 2:24, NKJV.
- "Beloved, I pray that you may prosper in all things and **be in health**, just as your soul prospers." 3 John 1:2, NKJV.

• CHAPTER 13 •

# How Can We Receive Healing?

IT IS GOD'S POWER to heal; there was the blood of Jesus has shed on the cross. We will decree it that we are healed. As I remind people to clean ourselves from all unrighteousness such as:

1. If we have not confessed our sins,
2. If we have disobedience heart in the Lord,
3. If we have unbelief heart,
4. If we have not forgiven others in the past!

These things can lead to blocking for healing in our bodies and our emotions. On some occasions, it could be really sin is the cause of sickness.

Any disease would take us to a point for examining our hearts. We enter into the presence of the Lord by prayer. Submitting our pain, our suffering, our discouragement, our past lay down on the Alter for the Lord Jesus.

We humble ourselves to draw near to Him, and He will draw near to us. The Holy Spirit will give us a fresh anointing to take us to the high level of closeness to His presence in the spirit.

When we study the Word of God and continually meditate upon His promise. We will build up our faith and declare in the healing scriptures.

We allow the Word of God to take-in into our inner spirit; it will create a good feeling of confidence. The beautiful things we must remember that Jesus has put himself in our place.

That we will not suffer or not having any sickness or no pain in this life, he paid the price for us. He suffered for us on the cross by giving his life. He shed His blood, which covered our sins, our guilt, our shame.

The Word said: we are believing in Christ because we have received Jesus as our Lord and Savior, we are a born-again Christian.

There is no condemnation or judgment for those who believe in Christ. Jesus put our name in the Book of Life. Ask ourselves, am I in Christ or not? If we are, so, we are free of sins, we are forgiven; we are healed by the blood of the Lamb of God.

Try to put our faith in the completed work of Jesus's sufferings. Our sins are forgiven, and our disease is transferred to Jesus. He took all of our guilt, our death.

He replaced it with a new life in himself. Jesus has already paid the price for your healing and has restored it into a new healthy life.

There is a unique joy with a new peace in Christ. He made it accessible to us by coming to the Father through Jesus the Son of God.

Now we recognize it, and it depends on us to acknowledge it and receive them all by faith that He has everything for us.

If we have a desire for ministers or elders of the church to pray in faith for us. They can lay hands on us and anoint us with an anointed oil.

The Word said the prayer of faith would save the sick person. If there is no manifestation of healing from the Lord, it is a natural thing to get discouraged.

But God loves faithful believers who ask and seek His face for an answer. We know that He is faithful. Let's check our hearts.

It might be, there is something that the Lord will reveal to us to repent our sins. We just declare the Word and believe the Word. He is watching over His promise; He is coming to touch our bodies; it's only a matter of time.

Continue praying and having faith in His Word. The most straightforward reason, we grow depressed and giving up our confidence.

We all love to have spontaneous healing, but often healings take place continually day by day. We have to be patient and being faithful in our beliefs.

We need to worship Jesus in a good time and in a bad time. We are praising Him for His marvelous work. Remember, He wants us to remain faithful to Him and to live in good health.

• CHAPTER 14 •

# How to become a Christian?

A CHRISTIAN WHO IS a follower of Jesus and trusts in him. The Bible gives a simple explanation so we can have a relationship with Him.

We will have a spiritual experience as we become born-again Christian believers. The great news of the Christian doctrine appears with the concept that God has chosen us.

He who formed us and created us in the image of His Son on this earth. I want just to take this opportunity to share how we can have a personal relationship with Jesus by faith.

It is essential to follow the way of God's Word is better than doing any other ritual Christianity. It will not help us to become Christian believers.

When we recognize that we have sinned against God, and our sin will separate us from God, and it will lead us to death.

We cannot make ourselves clean or forgive our own sins. He came to die on the cross for our iniquities; he sacrificed his life. He shed His blood for our sickness. Now we can go to Him by faith with no condemnation and no judgment.

Becoming a Christian is to have a simple faith in the Lord, learning His Word, allowing ourselves to have a fellowship with other Christian believers in the church.

Then we build up our confidence in the Word and living more in the peace of Christ. We grow into a better spiritual maturity in walking with the Lord.

When we move forward in faith, we develop our confidence in the Word of God only. Let's focus on this part that we **"believe"** that Jesus is the Son of God.

We are the sinners; we all need a Savior. He is the One who can save us from our sins. Now we repent our sins and accept Jesus into our hearts.

It is very simple to believe Jesus by faith. I will describe the few steps to remind us to make peace with our Heavenly Father, who loves us.

1. Believing in One true God and His Word
2. Repenting your sins
3. Inviting Jesus to come into your heart
4. Accepting Jesus as your Savior and Lord
5. To get baptized in water
6. Finding a Christian Fellowship to attend
7. Growing in the Spiritual life every day

When you follow these simple steps, you become a born-again Christian believer and welcome into God's family.

When you are devoting your time in His presence and studying the Word of God, then the Holy Spirit reveals Jesus to you. I am thrilled that you make the right decision to accept Jesus as your Savior.

According to the Bible, you are saved, and He will forgive all your sins and wipe out your tears and restore you from all your iniquity.

Then, remember your name is written in the Book of Life in heaven. I want to lead you a short prayer of salvation.

**Repeat after me:**

Heavenly Father, I thank you for your Son Jesus; you sent Him to die on the cross for me in my place. He rose again, and He is alive again.

I repent from all my sins; I invite Jesus to come into my heart; I believe Jesus as my Lord and my Savior. Thank you for caring for me and accepting me as a child of God. In Jesus' name. Amen.

# Conclusion

I will conclude this book by allowing me to serve you with the many greatest stories in the Bible.

In this book, we will see so many miracles and healing of God that have happened that we all be astonished.

I am glad I took this opportunity to search, and I summarized each story to make an inspiring message with the glorious name of God.

We will identify that God has been good to His people. It will inspire you by sharing the Word of God. It was a joy to present a demonstration of the power of God in every miracle and healing of God.

God acknowledged Himself in the Old Testament to the Israelites through phenomena events. Mostly, these miracles were to protect the Israelites.

They could survive past hardship, gone through difficulty, and overcame enemies. He has been a God of wonders and healing to those who asked Him.

He will answer them. The miracles of Jesus reveal to us that God is true. He cares for us, and He chooses us to be healthy. He desires us to live in health, prosperity, and peace.

He wants to renew our faith in a bountiful life. Jesus served us not only by healing many sick people.

But the Bible also mentioned everyone who went to Him. He turned no one away or not rejected anyone. The character of Jesus is to love and to heal every person who calls upon Jesus.

He is always ready to serve us; that's why He came down from heaven to save us and to heal our disease.

While Jesus did miracles for the people, they received healing and daily needs. He cared for the people with extreme love that He is eager to serve them today.

People had shown confidence in Him. Jesus worked wonders in the presence of the gathered people.

This book will sustain you, motivate you, and prepare you to grow into a mighty man or woman of God.

Sharing amazing stories about the men and women of God from the Bible can encourage us to continue being active in this life.

May this book serve you and refresh you to build up your faith in Christ. My dream is, this book will reach millions of Christian believers around the world.

Thank you for supporting me, and I am honored to serve you through this book, and may God bless you.

In the end, I would like to present my other books to you:
- **Parables of Jesus**
- **Wisely Decisions in Christ**
- **Manifestation of Prayer**
- **Encouraging Stories in the Bible**
- **Authority in the Bible**
- **Preaching with Fire**

# About the Author

DR. DANIEL KAZEMIAN HAS dedicated his life to the nonprofit organization International Evangelistic Ministry, to preach the Good News by the anointing of the Holy Spirit.

In June 1993, he was ordained to the ministry in the National Church of God by Dr. T. L. Lowery in Washington, DC. He has since become one of today's most dynamic charismatic preachers.

Christ walked into his life in January 1985, and Daniel was transformed into an exciting, enthusiastic dynamo for God.

He's passionate about sharing God's love and saving grace with everyone, as well as healing the sick. Daniel started his evangelistic career and his radio/TV ministry in Denmark-Scandinavia and abroad.

He is now serving in the prophetic and healing ministry, and he ministers in churches, seminars, conventions, crusades, and anywhere the Spirit of God leads him.

Daniel earned his associate degree from the National Bible College and Seminary in June 1993 in Fort Washington, Maryland, and a bachelor's degree, a master's degree, and a Doctor of Theology degree from the International Theological Seminary in July 1996 in Plymouth, Florida.

He is the president of the nonprofit organization, International Evangelistic Ministry, located in Gainesville, Georgia.

Contact him through email:
ieministry@hotmail.com

Visit our website:
www.InternationalEvangelisticMinistry.com

www.ingramcontent.com/pod-product-compliance
Lightning Source LLC
Chambersburg PA
CBHW060823050426
42453CB00008B/558